Living With Autism

Living With Autism
The Parents' Stories

by Kathleen M. Dillon, Ph.D.

Parkway Publishers, Inc.
Boone, North Carolina
1995

Parkway Publishers, Inc.
Box 3678
Boone, North Carolina 28607

First Printing 1995
Second Printing 1996

Library of Congress Cataloging-in-Publication Data

Dillon, Kathleen M., 1947-
    Living with autism : the parents' stories / by Kathleen M. Dillon.
        p.   cm.
    Includes bibliographical references and index.
    ISBN 0-9635752-7-9 (pbk.)
    1. Autism in children. 2. Autism in children—Case studies.
3. Autistic children—Family relationships. 4. Parents of autistic children—Interviews.
I. Title.

I dedicate this book to
Dennis Vogel
and to my parents,
Stella and Michael Hynek.

The Battlefield

I feel like a lone soldier lost on the battlefield of life. No one hears my silent cries. I have a great fear of death and an even greater fear of life. I constantly struggle to break through the steel armor and capture the spirit inside. I live one second at a time, sometimes I think I'm invincible. As tough as I try to be, something always manages to touch my heart and keep it soft and vulnerable. I have a solid steel faith in the future. I am physically stronger than anyone. I carry the weight of the entire world on my shoulders. I have mastered the art of suppressing raging anger. I hunger for knowledge that is unavailable. I have an overwhelming appreciation for the finer things in life; those things of highest quality: A sunset, a sunrise, a dewdrop on a blade of grass, a roaring thunderstorm, a mud puddle, clouds, and the touch of sand on bare feet. I am the most isolated person on earth. I am cast aside by my family and friends, yet admired and viewed reverently by them. I am the most selfish and most self-sacrificing person alive. I can laugh and know complete joy and simultaneously hold an ocean of tears. I have grieved more than a nation: I carry constant pain in my heart. I know true happiness is loving unconditionally, loving and not being loved back, a straight line, a meal that stays on the table, dry feet, circles, eyes looking to me not through me, a spoken word, any word, a response to a single command, a teardrop or silence. I am often criticized and pitied. I am not all that I can be or want to be. I keep searching the haunted castle of a beautiful mind. I am alone; I am the tiniest whisper in the thunderous echo of time. I am the parent of an autistic child.

Peggie Otero (1982)

(Reprinted with permission. Autism Society of America. Bethesda, MD. 1995)

CONTENTS

ILLUSTRATIONS

PREFACE

Childhood is a demanding and challenging period for all parents, and when a child has a problem, these demands and challenges are magnified. When the problem is autism, one of the most devastating and least understood mental disorders of childhood, it is hard to imagine how parents cope. This book is about autism as experienced by the parents of children with autism. It documents these parents' extraordinarily difficult odyssey. As one prominent researcher in the field of autism put it, "I think sometimes . . . the parents hurt more than the kids" (Lovaas, 1991).

In the preface to his book, *Awakenings*, Oliver Sacks (1990) wrote: There were always two books, potentially, demanded by every clinical experience: one more purely medical or classical—an objective description of disorders, mechanisms, syndromes; the other more existential and personal—an empathic entering into the patients experiences and worlds (p. xxxvi). I have tried to include both of these books in this volume. The first part of this book is a review of the professional literature, summarizing empirically and scientifically presented experiences of parents of individuals with autism. The second part is a series of personal interviews with parents of individuals with autism; these are real-life illustrations of what it is like to live this life. The scientific studies provide us with the most reliable information about autism, and the anecdotal accounts serve as useful illustrations of the reality of living with autism, as well as sources for new hypotheses to explain and treat the disorder.

In the personal interview chapters of this book, you will read excerpts of interviews with the parents of some individuals with autism. The interviews were confidentially arranged through Community Resources for People with Autism, in Northampton, Massachusetts. In each case, a professional diagnosis of autism was made independently. An open-ended questionnaire was used (see Appendix A), modified by the responses of the parent. For example, if a parent said that his or her child did not speak, the remaining questions on speech were, obviously, eliminated.

Questions about areas which the parent said were not a problem were also eliminated. In addition, parents were encouraged to digress or elaborate as they saw fit. The interviews each took approximately three hours.

The cases presented here were selected to represent children with autism of a variety of ages, of both sexes, of different types of abilities and symptoms, and of different degrees of improvement. This sample also represents a wide variety of parental ages (from 20's to late 40's), of types of family structure (including traditional, adopted, foster, and single-parent headed by mother or father), of parental level of education (ranging from high school to advanced degrees), and of types of parental occupation (blue collar to professional).

Some limitations should be noted. The sample is neither random nor exhaustive. Parental impressions were sampled at one point in time and do not necessarily reflect how the individual with autism would be seen today by the parents. The opinion of one parent may or may not be shared by the other parent. Lastly, the interview focused on the autistic behavior of the individual and should, therefore, not be considered a complete biography.

Although all the interviews were taped, transcribed, edited, and then checked for accuracy, it is possible that errors are present, and the author accepts full responsibility for them. Words in brackets have been added to smooth transitions and improve readability. All names, dates, and places have been purposely changed to protect identities. All parents agreed to release this information in the hopes of helping others.

This is not a positive, everything-will-be-all-right book about autism. Rather, this is a book that acknowledges the seriousness of this disorder and the immense challenges faced by parents of children with autism. It does not, however, paint a picture devoid of satisfaction or hope. The ability of parents to survive and to derive meaning from this suffering is, in itself, a truly remarkable story.

When Derrick Bell's book on racist America, *Faces at the Bottom of the Well*, was described as unremittingly despairing, Bell responded: "No, you don't understand. For a black person in this society, the truth is never despairing. It reaffirms that it is not their fault. It is an affirmation of themselves and not a basis for despair" (Greenhouse, 1992, p. 7). In this book, I hope to reveal some truths about autism from the parent's perspective, to reaffirm the message that it is not the parents' fault, and to provide some incredible stories of courage and coping.

In addition to supporting parents of children with autism, this book is for the families and friends of those parents, to help them understand what the parents are experiencing, in the hope that they may be more empathic and supportive. This book is also useful to professionals and paraprofessionals who work with families of individuals with autism, or who teach others to work with such families. It may help them ensure that they are not inadvertently adding to the burdens of parents who are already stressed to the maximum. These professionals include pediatricians, neurologists, psychologists, social workers, communication specialists, special education teachers, teacher aides, occupational therapists, physical therapists, respite workers, dentists, and lawyers. Finally, this book is intended for policy makers and government officials at local, state, and national levels, who have the power to help or hurt these parents by voting on research and policies affecting people with autism.

I would like to acknowledge Western New England College, in Springfield, MA, for funding this project through their Summer Research Grant Program; Community Resources for People with Autism, in Northampton, MA, for assistance in contacting parents to interview; and, especially, the parents I interviewed, for sharing their time and the most personal details of their lives. I am grateful to the Autism Society of America for giving me permission to reproduce Peggy Otero's "The Battlefield" and the illustrations depicting the characteristics of persons with autism. I would like to thank Lahri Bond for his informative illustrations. Michael LeClerc took my photograph that appears on the backcover of this book. Finally, I express my appreciation to Nora Muller who edited my manuscript.

Living With Autism

Chapter 1
Review of the Professional Literature

What is Autism?

Autism is a biologically caused mental disorder appearing early in life and, usually, persisting in some form throughout life. This disorder can appear in many different forms. For example: some individuals with autism will be verbal, while others will be mute; some will have subnormal intelligence, while others will have normal intelligence. All individuals with autism, however, will have in common three serious impairments involving their social interaction, their ability to communicate, and their patterns of behavior.

This core set of impairments is defined in a book of diagnostic criteria for mental disorders, *The Diagnostic and Statistical Manual of Mental Disorders,* which is published by the American Psychiatric Association (currently in its fourth edition, it is commonly referred to as the DSM-IV). The diagnostic system in this book is recognized by the majority of health professionals and insurance companies. According to the DSM-IV, to be diagnosed as having Autistic Disorder, an individual must have a minimum of 6 of the 12 problems listed below, and the onset of these problems must be prior to three years of age (American Psychiatric Association [APA], 1994).

Impairment in social interaction due to autism is evident if an individual has two or more of the following problems:

> Marked impairment in the use of multiple nonverbal behaviors, such as eye-to-eye gaze, facial expression, body postures, and gestures to regulate social interaction.

Failure to develop peer relationships appropriate to developmental level.

A lack of spontaneous seeking to share enjoyment, interests, or achievement with other people.

Lack of social or emotional reciprocity.

Impairment in communication due to autism is evident if an individual has at least one of the following problems:

Delay in, or total lack of, the development of spoken language (not accompanied by an attempt to compensate through alternative modes of communication, such as gesture or mime).

In individuals with adequate speech, marked impairment in the ability to initiate or sustain conversation with others.

Stereotyped and repetitive use of language, or idiosyncratic language.

Lack of varied, spontaneous make-believe play or social imitative play appropriate to developmental level.

Impairment in patterns of behavior due to autism is evident if an individual has at least one of the following problems:

Encompassing preoccupation with one or more stereotyped and restricted patterns of interests which are abnormal in either intensity or focus.

Apparently inflexible adherence to specific, nonfunctional routines or rituals.

Stereotyped and repetitive motor mannerisms.

Persistent preoccupation with parts of objects (pp.70-71).

As a learning companion to the DSM-IV, the American Psychiatric Association publishes a book of real cases, focusing on the information necessary to make a diagnosis (Spitzer, Gibbon, Skodol, Williams, & First, 1994). One of the cases illustrating Autistic Disorder is called Echo. In this case, 3½-year-old Richard shows examples of all three core impairments. His social interaction impairment is evident in that he fails to greet his parents when he sees them and in his lack of interest in other children, including his younger brother. His communication is also limited; he echoes other speech when he needs to communicate. For example, he will say, "Do you want a drink?", when he wants a drink. He is also aloof and not interested in playing typical baby games with his parents. Thirdly, he has peculiar patterns of behavior. He flaps his arms when excited, and he has a limited number of interests, consisting primarily of doing puzzles and making patterns with kitchen utensils while holding a miniature car. He never plays imaginatively with this car, but he insists on holding it, day and night. Trying to remove the car from his hand results in temper tantrums lasting an hour or more, with screaming, kicking, and biting of himself and others. His parents noticed peculiarities in his behavior from the time he was only a few months old.

In addition to the three core areas of impairment required for diagnosis of autism, the DSM-IV outlines a number of other characteristics that may be found in a child with autism, including:

Mental retardation.
Uneven profile of cognitive skills.
Language comprehension less than vocabulary
    suggests.
Hyperactivity.
Short attention span.
Impulsivity.
Aggressiveness.
Self-injurious behaviors (e.g.: head banging; or finger, hand, or wrist biting).
Temper tantrums (usually in young children).
High threshold for pain.
Exaggerated reactions to lights or odors.

Fascination with certain stimuli.
Abnormalities in eating (e.g.: diet limited to a few
        foods, or eating inedible substances).
Sleep disorders.
Giggling or weeping for no apparent reason.
No emotion when it is warranted.
Lack of fear or excessive fear.
Depression (in adolescents who are aware of their
        disorder) (APA, 1994, pp. 67-68).

In short, autism is a serious mental disorder involving a significant range and number of defects which have a major impact
on the day-to-day functioning and development of the individual
and which present enormous challenges for the caretakers.

Difficulties with Diagnosis

For the parents of autistic children, the difficulties begin very early.
Some children begin to have symptoms in the first few days of
their lives, and some parents, especially those who have had other
children, immediately suspect a problem (even though current
medical tests are often unable to detect it). Other children appear to
start off normally and then regress into autism. It is common for
the parents to notice something odd about their child, although
they can't quite figure out what it is. Maybe their child stiffens
when they try to hold it or doesn't seem to pay attention to them
when they speak. Maybe their child doesn't respond to them by
smiling or seems either very cranky or very docile. In a study done
of home movies taken by parents of children before the age of two,
and before the children were diagnosed as autistic, a number of
early signs were evident, some as early as the first few months of
life (Adrien et al., 1991). In one study, 1½ was the average child's
age when parents reported concerns to their pediatrician, with the
age range spreading from 6 months to 2½ years (Siegel, Pliner,
Escher, & Elliott, 1988).

Although labelling an individual is often considered demean-
ing, when one is faced with the perplexing symptoms of autism, it
is comforting to have a label. It is a starting point, even if the label

is negative. Autism, however, is often not diagnosed until long after the parents' first suspicion. Children with autism often do not receive initial evaluations before age 2, and do not receive a diagnosis of autism until around $4^1/_2$ (Siegel et al., 1988).

Typically, the pediatrician first tells the parents not to worry, that the child's behavior is within the range of normalcy. There is, in fact, a wide range of normal development for infants and, more often than not, when pediatricians hear vague complaints, they are correct in dismissing them. Autism is, after all, a very rare disorder. It is estimated that only 4 or 5 out of 10,000 births will result in the full syndrome of autism. This means there are only about 110,000 people in the United States with the full syndrome, one third of whom are children (and 80% of whom are boys) (Powers, 1989b). The parents may not have previously heard of or known anyone with this condition, and the pediatrician also may have not previously treated anyone with autism. But the parents who live with the child, and witness a multitude of instances of odd behavior, will, typically, return again with the same complaints.

At this point, the pediatrician may persist in his or her original dismissal and imply that the parents may have a problem—that they want a perfect baby, or that they are over-anxious parents, or, if this is their first child, that they are simply ignorant of what babies are like. Again, pediatricians are often correct in this assessment. Parents of children with autism, at this point, may start to doubt their own parenting abilities (Cutler & Kozloff, 1987). Usually, however, the parents persist, trusting their gut instinct that something is amiss. They return to the pediatrician, who, either because he or she has finally decided that something may indeed be wrong or simply out of frustration, begins referring the child to specialists for further evaluations. Typically, the pediatrician starts by ruling out more common, more easily treatable disorders. For example, if the child in question is not talking at all, or talking incoherently at an age where most children are beginning to speak, the pediatrician may refer the child for hearing tests. Usually, the parents suspect that this is not the real problem because they have seen their child respond to some sounds, if not their voices. Pediatricians, however, want to be sure they have ruled out all other possibilities before they diagnose children as having something as serious as autism.

Fig. 1: Difficulties With Diagnosis

The following tests are recommended before a diagnosis of autism is reached: a family history, including instances of autism or similar disorders (e.g., mental retardation); a history of the pregnancy and birth, and the child's medical history; a detailed physical examination (including certain specifics, such as a careful examination of the skin, which might reveal tuberous sclerosis); a general, age-appropriate medical and neurodevelopmental examination; a psychological evaluation by a clinical psychologist who understands autism and knows what tests are appropriate; and a laboratory work-up, including a chromosomal analysis, an MRI or CAT scan, a cerebral spinal fluid examination, an auditory brain stem response, an ophthalmological examination, a hearing test, a blood test (for phenylalanine, uric acid, pyruvic acid, and evidence of herpes infection), and a 24-hour urine examination for a metabolic screen and for the level of uric acid and calcium. It may take many frustrating months, and even years, of this type of testing before the parents learn their child has the disorder of autism. Yet children who receive early intervention tend to have better communication skills and fewer out-of-control behaviors, and parents of these children often have a greater understanding and acceptance of their child's disorder (Caramagno, 1992).

Confusion Over Labelling

There are a number of questions regarding terminology which, when left unanswered, can add to the confusion and frustration of parents. Is autism a mental or organic disorder? How can a child be considered autistic if he or she is not withdrawn? What is the difference between a pervasive developmental disorder and an autistic disorder? Can children who are autistic also be mentally retarded? Is childhood schizophrenia the same as childhood autism?

At one time, mental health professionals tried to clearly separate mental disorders, which were defined as having psychological causes, from organic disorders, which were defined as having physiological causes. This distinction has blurred in recent years, as research evidence has challenged the validity of it. As the DSM-IV states: "there is much 'physical' in 'mental' disorders and much 'mental' in 'physical' disorders" (APA, 1994, p. xxi). Today, a mental disorder is defined as a "clinically significant behavioral or psychological syndrome or pattern that occurs in an individual and that is associated with present distress or disability or with a significant increased risk of suffering death, pain, disability, or an important loss of freedom. . . . Whatever its original cause, it must currently be considered a manifestation of a behavioral, psychological, or biological dysfunction in the individual" (APA, 1994, pp. xxi-xxii). In this system, autism is considered a mental disorder caused by an organic, specifically neurological, dysfunction.

Fig. 2: Confusion Over Labelling

There is also confusion about the word *autistic*. This word is used to refer to a cluster of symptoms, also known as a syndrome; it is also used to mean simply withdrawn. To be classified as having an autistic disorder, a child must have the symptoms outlined in the DSM-IV and listed earlier in this book. But to say someone is autistic could just mean that the person is withdrawn from others. Although many children who have an autistic disorder are also withdrawn, they do not need to be withdrawn to be classified as having autism. When the word *autistic* is used by itself, it is not always clear whether what is meant is the full syndrome or a single characteristic.

In the DSM-IV, under the chapter, "Disorders Usually First Evident in Infancy, Childhood, or Adolescence," is the category,

"Pervasive Developmental Disorder (PDD)." This group of disorders is defined by "severe and pervasive impairment in several areas of development: reciprocal social interaction skills, communication skills, or the presence of stereotyped behavior, interests, and activities" (APA, 1994, p. 65).

Autistic Disorder falls in the PDD category, as do four other disorders: Rett's Disorder, Childhood Disintegrative Disorder, Asperger's Disorder, and Pervasive Developmental Disorder Not Otherwise Classified. This last category is used, in part, to classify atypical cases of autism, i.e., cases that do not meet all the previously discussed criteria for autism because of late age of onset, atypical symptomatology, or subthreshold symptomology.

A number of psychologists and psychiatrists have been debating whether or not Pervasive Developmental Disorder is a useful term. Some say the term is "an inappropriate and uninformative" term that "does not take advantage of the hard-won public awareness of autism" (Happe & Frith, 1991, p. 1167). Others oppose the use of the term on the grounds that those who are labelled as PDD, rather than autistic, may be deprived of their lawful rights because fewer people are aware that PDD indicates a serious mental disorder, as compared with the number who understand what autism implies (Gillberg, 1991). The President of the Autism Society of America argues that those diagnosed as having PDD, instead of autism, may be denied their lawful rights: "Autism was recently added to the list of handicapping conditions in the federal laws mandating special education. PDD does not have this status" ("Changes Requested," 1991, p. 14). On the other hand, some professionals prefer to keep the term PDD, arguing that changing the term would involve considerable cost in terms of educating parents, service agencies, and other professionals (Volkmar & Cohen, 1991).

Unfortunately, this professional debate over, and inconsistent use of, various terms for this condition only adds to the confusion of parents already bewildered by the perplexing behaviors of their child. The standard today is that a child whose behavior meets all the criteria outlined in the DSM-IV for Autistic Disorder is considered to have autism, and that autism is one of a number of pervasive developmental disorders.

Another confusion with diagnosis has to do with the relationship between autism and mental retardation. A number of parents remarked to the author that at least their child (who had been diagnosed with autism or PDD) was not retarded, when, in fact, their child was retarded. The fact is that, while it is true that not all people with autism test in the retarded range on IQ tests (below 70), the majority of them (66%) do. Only 16% achieve scores in the average range or higher (90 or above). Individuals who score above 70 are sometimes called "high-functioning" autistics (Phelps & Grabowski, 1991). However, even high-functioning autistics experience deficits that are not usually found in normal individuals (Yirmiya & Sigman, 1991). "It cannot be overemphasized that all psychiatric diagnoses may co-occur with . . . mental retardation" (Popper & Steingard, 1994, p. 781). In the case of autism, over half of all individuals diagnosed with Autistic Disorder as their primary diagnosis will have a concurrent diagnosis of Mental Retardation. Other problems that have been observed occurring with autism include mood and anxiety disorders.

Yet another confusion is between Childhood Autism and Childhood Schizophrenia. These are very different disorders. The prominent feature of schizophrenia is the presence of delusions or hallucinations. Neither of these occur in Autistic Disorder.

Unanswered Questions of Cause

Once parents learn that their child has autism, a natural question that arises is: How did this happen? Once again, the parents are not likely to get simple or satisfying responses from professionals. This has to do, in large part, with the present limits of medical science. There may be no abnormalities observed during the pregnancy or birth. The child, at birth, may appear perfectly normal, and the physical body may be perfectly normal; that is to say, the results of all the tests done on a person during a physical examination will often be normal. Indeed, in many cases, even sophisticated computerized tests will not pick up any signs of abnormality (Zilbovicius et al., 1992). At one time, not that long ago, it was assumed that, because there were no obvious physical abnormalities, the disorder must be caused by faulty nurturing on the part of the parents (Sanua, 1986a), especially the mother, hence the term "refrigerator mother." Fortunately, that opinion is no longer accepted by the vast majority of professionals in the U.S. (though it can still be found here, and is more common in Europe) (Sanua, 1986b). Nonetheless, parents are often given only vague and equivocal answers to questions regarding the cause of their child's condition.

Fig. 3: Unanswered Questions of Cause

Professionals today see autism as a behavioral disorder with an organic cause. Many of them also accept that there are many different organic causes that can result in the same outcome. Autism has been associated with encephalitis, phenylketonuria, tuberos sclerosis, anoxia during birth, and maternal rubella (APA, 1994). In one study, twelve rare diseases known to cause central nervous system pathology were found in 11% of a group of individuals with autism (Ritvo et al., 1990).

In other cases, the disorder appears to have a possible genetic origin. In one review of the literature, it was stated that, 36% of identical twins shared a diagnosis of autism, compared to 0% of fraternal twins. Also, children born to parents who already had a child with autism were much more likely to have autism than children born to parents of nonautistic children. Between 5% and 25% of the siblings of individuals with autism experience problems such as delays in learning (Popper & Steingard, 1994). In a small number of cases (less than 5%), a clear cut genetic anomaly, called Fragile X, has been observed (Rutter, 1991).

The possibility of a link between environmental toxins and autism has also been suggested. One example is in Leominster, Massachusetts, where 22 cases of autism have been identified in families that live, or have lived, near a toxic site (formerly a Foster Grant sunglasses manufacturing plant) ("Toxic waste," 1990). Researchers, however, have failed to find genetic abnormalities, using standard karyotyping methods, on 14 children with autism who had one or both parents growing up near the plastics site for five or more consecutive years. At this point in time, it appears premature to conclude that environmental toxins can contribute to autism, or to rule out this relationship (Spiker, Lotspeich, Hallmayer, Kraemer, & Ciaranello, 1993).

Some professionals, have suggested that there may, in fact, be more than one disorder here, and have tentatively proposed a sub-classification system based on different behavioral problems (Castelloe & Dawson, 1993; Fotheringham, 1991). It is hoped that, when the causes of autism are better understood, and the area or type of brain damage is more clearly defined, a classification system can be devised using these factors.

Because professionals cannot, in many cases, answer the question of cause, parents are left with this question unanswered, as well as the question of whether or not they should risk having more children. Although autism is an extremely rare disorder, which may, in some cases, have been caused by environmental factors, in most cases this cannot be known for sure. Parents will inevitably consider the possibility that subsequent children might be autistic or have other problems. Not only, then, are parents left with not knowing what caused autism in one child, they are also left with the responsibility of making a necessarily uninformed decision about future children.

Grief and Sorrow

Any loss involving a child is traumatizing. There is no relationship more intimate than the one between a parent and a child, and feelings of attachment begin even before the child is born. Parents often fantasize about how their child will look or act, projecting their own hopes and dreams onto the child (Rando, 1986). When parents learn that their child has autism and come to accept the diagnosis and its implications, they begin the process of mourning, both for the child who will never be and for the present losses in the child with autism. The mourning for a child who has died is considered to be one of the most severe types of grief. However, this grief is usually resolved, albeit over a long period of time. The mourning for an child with autism may never be totally resolved, because the presence of the disability serves as a constant reminder of the loss. Some researchers have referred to this type of mourning as *chronic sorrow* (Burke, Hainsworth, Eakes, & Lindgren, 1992).

This chronic sorrow can vary in intensity throughout the life span of the child, often increasing in severity at times when anticipated developmental milestones are not reached. For example: when other children of the same age are out playing, the child with autism may be engaging in solitary play, not playing at all, or distressed by playing; when other teenagers are dating and driving cars, the teenager with autism may be uninterested in the opposite sex and unable to drive; when other adult children are leaving the nest, getting married, and having children, the son or daughter with autism may have no friends and be still dependent on the parents. A person with autism may not reach many major milestones "on time," or may not reach them at all. There are also many smaller accomplishments, which most people take for granted, over which the parents of a child with autism agonize. For example, one 15-

year-old boy just said, "Hello," as a greeting, for the first time. He had been speaking for many years, but, instead of greeting others when they said, "Hello," he would oddly purse his lips and turn away. As the characteristic problems of autism are often severe and pervasive, so too will be the sorrow over these losses.

Fig. 4: Grief and Sorrow

Trials of Day-to-Day Living

While parents may have problems with professionals over the diagnosis, labelling, or cause of their child's autism, nothing compares with the stress of living day to day with a person with autism. No one who hasn't been through it, not even the most empathetic friend, can fully understand this experience. One way to get a realistic idea of the stress involved would be to spend an unstructured day alone with a person with autism.

As was mentioned earlier, children with autism share a common diagnosis, along with the general traits outlined in the DSM-IV criteria, but no two children with autism will manifest these problems in the same way.

> In looking at a cross section of individuals with autism, probably the most striking initial impression is of tremendous variability. The sample would include some infants and some old men, some eccentric piano tuners with IQs of 110 and some profoundly retarded, institutionalized individuals. Some gentle wraithlike 7 year-old might be observed, as would some screeching adolescent who banged his head to the point of skull fracture. A few individuals with idiosyncratic interests in train or bus schedules would be present, as would many individuals who appeared unable or unwilling to communicate. (Volkmar & Cohen, 1988, p. 71)

Indeed, these authors state that it was incredible, as well as fortunate, that Leo Kanner (1943) was able, from such a mixed bag of symptoms, to first identify the syndrome.

Because of this extreme variability, the stories in this book will never be matched exactly by other children, although similarities will be observed. Some of the behaviors exhibited by children with autism are in the realm of delayed development, in the sense that they are characteristic of much younger children. For example, a teenage boy may reach for your hand to cross a street, much as a young child might. Some of the behaviors, however, are unusual for any age, and some are bizarre. For example, a young girl with autism, when asked a simple question, may respond by flapping her hands in front of her face.

Because the three core areas of impairment cover such a wide range of activities, some professionals have devised continuums, ranking categories of activities from the most severe to the mildest. The following continuum for communication impairments, by Lorna Wing (1988), is an example:

There may be complete absence of desire to communicate with others.

At a less severe level, needs are expressed, but there
is no other form of communication.

Those with speech may make factual comments, but
these are not part of a social exchange, and they
are often irrelevant to the social context.

Some older children and adults talk a great deal, but
do not engage in true reciprocal conversation.
Instead, they ask questions repetitively, or
deliver lengthy monologues, regardless of the
content of the conversation, the response of the
listener, or indications by the listener of boredom or desire to leave (p. 94).

The Autism Society of America has also enumerated diagnostic criteria, accompanied by stick-figure sketches of the behavior,
which may be helpful in aiding recognition. (See Fig. 5)

Another way symptoms of autism can be rated is on a scale,
such as the Childhood Autism Rating Scale (CARS). In this scale,
15 areas of functioning are scored from (1), indicating age appropriate or normal, to (4), indicating severely abnormal. This
scale rates abnormalities in the following areas: relating to people;
imitation; emotional response; body use; object use; adaptation to
change; visual response; listening response; taste, smell, and touch
response and use; fear or nervousness; verbal communication; nonverbal communication; activity level; level and consistency of
intellectual response; and general impression (Schopler, Reichler,
& Renner, 1986).

Uta Frith (1993) has theorized that one major cognitive deficit
may account for all the problem behaviors. Her evidence suggests
that individuals with autism do not have "the ability to think about
thought or to imagine another individual's state of mind" (p. 112).
Frith sees this ability as automatic in normal people, and a prereq-
uisite to the abilities to engage in imaginative ideas, to interpret
feelings, and to understand intentions beyond the literal content of
speech (like those found in humor and irony)—activities that seem

difficult or impossible for people with autism. A corroborating study concluded that, for the majority of people with autism, there may be insufficient development of a theory of mind. Only for a minority (approximately 20-30%) may this theory of mind develop, by the teenage years, to the equivalent of a normal child three or four years old, and for some of these, to that of a child six or seven years old, but often only by adulthood (Holroyd & Baron-Cohen, 1993).

AUTISM:

Fig. 5: Characteristics Exhibited by Persons With Autism

(Reprinted with permission. Autism Society of America. Bethesda, MD. 1995)

Scientific reports provide the most verifiable, and therefore acceptable, accounts of autistic behavior, but anecdotal reports by parents can also provide examples of what one might expect as a parent, as well as provide researchers with further opportunities for study and understanding.

Short accounts by parents are presented in every issue of *The Advocate* (newsletter of the Autism Society of America, Inc.). A collection of these stories has also been published as a book (Sposato, n.d.), and individual parents have also written book-length accounts of their experiences. One potential problem with these accounts, however, is that they do not always include a certified, professional diagnosis of autism. For example, some of the children whom parents claim are high-functioning appear to have Asperger's Disorder rather than Autistic Disorder.

It should be noted that no group of people is exempt from having a child with autism. Beverly Sills Greenough (1989) wrote about her experiences as a parent in the foreword to *Children with Autism, A Parents' Guide,* by Michael Powers. William Christopher (1989), better known as Father Mulcahy from the movie and TV show, MASH, along with his wife, Barbara, wrote about their adopted son, in *Mixed Blessings.* And Sylvester Stallone, who has a son with autism, has established the Stallone Foundation in Culver City, California, to fund research into autism.

Personal accounts by individuals with autism offer a rare inside view of the world of autism. One especially interesting first-person account is the short, but revealing autobiography of Tony W. (Volkmar & Cohen, 1985). Here is the opening paragraph:

> I was living in a world of daydreaming and Fear revolving aboud my self I had no care about Human feelings or other people. I was afraid of everything! I was terrified to go in the water swimming. [and of] loud noises; in the dark I had severe, repetitive Nightmares and occasionally hearing electronic noises with nightmares. I would wake up so terrified and disoriented I wasnt able to Find my way out of the room for a few miniuts. It felt like I was being draged to Hell. I was afraid of simple things

such as going into the shower, getting my nails cliped, soap in my eyes, rides in the carnival-except the Spook house I love it, I allso like Hellish envirments such as spookhouses at the Carnival, Halloween, and movies-horror. I rember Yale Child Study Ctr. I ignored the doctors and did my own thing such as make something and played or idolize it not caring that anybody was in the room. I ws also very hat[e]full and sneakey. I struggled and breathed hard because I wanted to kill the gunia pig; as soon as the examiner turned her back I killed it. I hated my mother becaus she try to stop me from being in my world and doing what I liked; so I stoped and as soon as she turned her back I went at it agen. I was very Rebellious and sneaky and distructive. I would plot to kill my mother and destroy the world. Evil things astonsihed me such as an H. bomb. I loved cartoons and their envirments. I also [had] a very warp sence of humor and learn[ed] perveted thing[s] verryquickly. I used to lash out of controll and repeat sick, perverted Phrases as well as telling people violent, wild, untrue things to impres them (pp. 49-50).

Tony was studied at Yale, and his diagnosis of autism was confirmed by Volkmar and Cohen, two experts in the field of autism. Other autobiographical accounts of individuals claiming to have autism are more questionable. For example, the best-selling *Nobody Nowhere* (Williams, 1992), and its sequel, *Somebody Somewhere* (Williams, 1994), present the case of Donna Williams, who often appears to suffer more from the aftermath of abuse than she does from autism.

Movies are another source of information about what autism is like. Although Dustin Hoffman's portrayal of a man with autism in the movie, *Rainman* (Johnson & Levinson, 1988), is uncannily familiar to anyone who has been in the company of an individual with autism, and although this movie undoubtedly helped to educate the public about autism, it also helped to perpetuate a myth about the disorder—namely, that people with autism also possess one or more islands of genius.

The reality, however, is that the vast majority of people with autism are not savants. The total number of known prodigious savants with autism or other types of disorders, in the world, is less than 100 cases in the last 100 years. Some individuals with autism do have better memories for some events, but they would not be considered prodigies. The other myth which must be dispelled is that being savant will somehow make up for other deficits. One type of savant talent is to be able to mentally calculate the day on which a specified date falls (e.g., to be able to figure out on what day of the week February 21, 1913 fell). Although this is done remarkably quickly by people who are calendar calculators, there is little use for this talent, other than entertainment, and the individuals often remain retarded in their day-to-day functioning. One perspective on savants is that they have memory problems, rather than skills, because they cannot forget trivial or meaningless information (Treffert, 1989).

The most important thing to realize is that autistic behaviors do not happen in a vacuum. They happen in a family system and, therefore, they affect family life. For example, if a child with autism does not sleep through most of the night, then the sleep of the parents will be affected. Who has not heard the tired lament of parents of a normal newborn, who, during the first few weeks or months, does not sleep through the night. Imagine having an child with autism, who, for the first ten years or more of his or her life, not only does not sleep during much of the night, but also spends that time yelling, singing, repeating conversations, climbing, knocking over furniture, roaming around the house, and/or trying to leave the house. Many parents of these children have them sleep in a room with just a mattress, and lock them in at night for their own safety. The parents of these children virtually never get a good night's sleep while the children are with them, and having the children sleep anywhere but in their own homes is, more or less, impossible.

Some of the most disturbing behaviors of individuals with autism involve their being aggressive toward themselves or others.

Fig. 6: Trials of Day-to-Day Living

A very minor event (e.g., saying "I know") can set off some children with autism into wild, screaming, pinching, biting, and/or throwing frenzies, which can last for an hour or more. There is great power in pathology, and many parents find themselves yielding to autistic demands in order to avoid these episodes, creating, in the process, a bizarre family life (Holmes & Carr, 1991). Sometimes, however, there appears to be no reason for the behavior, and little parents can do once it begins, other than wait for the child to fatigue. The Christophers experienced this type of behavior with their son, Ned:

> There would be outbursts of this terrible [violent] behavior. . . . Absolutely nothing worked—-the cold shoulders, pleas, threats, withdrawing privileges—- nothing at all. . . . In order to protect herself from Ned's attacks while allowing him some freedom, Barbara would lock herself in our bedroom. When she had to be in his presence, she now wore a heavy coat buttoned to the chin (Christopher & Christopher, 1989, pp. 151-152).

Even the behavior of so-called high-functioning individuals with autism can be maddening on a day-to-day basis. Most people with siblings can remember either tormenting brothers or sisters by saying some derogatory phrase over and over again, or enduring having it done to them. Indeed, one form of psychological torture consists of the monotonous, repeated presentation of a sensory event over a long period of time. Yet the repetitive stating of the same phrases or stories is a common occurrence for some individuals with autism. The event may have occurred many years before, and the individual may have told you the same story ten times a day for the last few years. Indeed, he or she may have just told you the same story a minute ago. It doesn't matter; the person with autism will tell it to you again, as if for the first time. Also, it makes no difference if you ignore the person, give subtle hints that you are not interested, or even tell the person directly that you have heard the story before; the individual with autism will persist in telling you again.

The hardest thing to appreciate, if you are not the parent of an autistic child, is the relentless nature of the symptoms of autism. We all use certain expressions to illustrate emotional intensity, such as, "If I've told you once, I've told you a thousand times," and we may, therefore, conclude that, when these parents talk about certain behaviors occurring thousands of times, they don't literally mean that, but are just using that expression to emphasize how irritatingly often something occurs. The truth of the matter is that, in fact, many behaviors can and do occur that often. Imagine a record stuck on the same phrase; then imagine having to listen to it for an hour, a day, a week, a year. Now maybe you will be somewhat closer to appreciating the plight of parents of children with autism. To give you a specific example: in a recent study, a boy with autism said, "Can I talk?", 618 times during one 3-hour period of observation (Coggins & Frederickson, 1988).

Any one of the behaviors mentioned can be extremely disturbing to the people who have to live with it. Now multiply that one behavior by six or more. This is the minimum number of atypical behaviors found in most individuals with autism. One doctor, in describing schizophrenia, also characterized autism:

> I guess the way I think of schizophrenia is as an illness; it's a total picture. It's not like a peculiarity of

behavior. It's not as if someone has an idiosyncracy or has some peculiar way of doing things or thinking things. Schizophrenia is an involvement of a person in an illness. There are abnormalities of behavior, abnormalities of thinking, abnormalities of feeling, abnormalities of the way people move across a room. There are peculiarities in what people perceive. There seems to be a very global impairment of what we think of as the highest psychological functioning, the most intricate, sophisticated, complex psychological functioning that people have (Sage, 1984).

Some professionals feel that, because individuals with autism fail so often, they tend toward a state of learned helplessness, which may further depress their motivation to learn. The challenge for educators, therapists, and parents is to avoid or minimize opportunities for failure, while finding meaningful reinforcers. This is a colossal challenge.

One suggestion is that interspersing already-mastered maintenance tasks with new tasks being taught may reduce the learner's sense of failure (Koegel & Mentis, 1985). Unusual forms of reinforcement have also been suggested. One behavioral principle is that high-frequency behaviors can be reinforcing. For individuals with autism, these behaviors might include delayed echolalia (repeating words heard, but after a period of time, sometimes even years), perseveration (repeating the same phrase over and over again), and stereotypies (repeating the same behavior over and over again). In one study, these behaviors were used as reinforcers for low-frequency, desired behaviors, the rationale being that what may be reinforcing for other children (such as toys, praise, smiles, or approval) may not be reinforcing for children with autism. One reinforcer was allowing the child to say, "Eat your beef stew!"; another was allowing him to repeat, "See 'n Say" over and over; and a third was letting a child wave her hands in front of her eyes (Charlop, Kurtz, & Casey, 1990). In another study, visual movement (specifically, being able to use windshield wipers) was used as the reinforcer (Rincover, Newsom, Lovaas, & Koegel, 1977).

These reinforcers successfully helped these children learn various tasks, such as discriminating between *same* and *different*, and adding up coins to a requested amount.

In addition to disturbing behavioral symptoms, some individuals with autism also have related medical problems, most commonly seizures, which are most likely to be a problem for low-functioning individuals. They often first appear in adolescence (Volkmar, 1989), and can vary from mild, detectable only by an electroencephalogram, to violent, with possible fever and loss of consciousness (Hart, 1993).

Trying to Get Adequate Treatment

Since the advent of deinstitutionalization in the 1960's, the burden of finding adequate treatment has fallen on the parents. Today courts will authorize residential school referrals only in the most extreme cases. Although private residential schools are available, they can be very expensive, and they are not always in the best interests of the child. What parents need to do is learn what laws, at the state and federal levels, apply to their child's education, and to make sure their child receives all the services to which he or she is entitled. All children with disabilities or learning problems are entitled to special education, with an individualized education plan, between the ages of 3 and 21 (Hart, 1993). However, it may take some very assertive behavior on the parents' part for a child with autism to actually receive this. Joseph and Joyce Marshall, parents of a girl with autism and officers of an Autism Society of America chapter in Tennessee, give this advice to parents:

> When you find out what's due you, demand it. You
> may have to get mean. I'd be surprised if you didn't
> have to get mean. It doesn't make you real popular
> with the local school system, but you get results. If
> you don't fight for the rights of your child, no one
> else will (Autism Society of America [ASA], 1992).

Some suggestions on how to get insurance companies to cover the costs of treatment are outlined in *Let Me Hear Your Voice: A Family's Triumph Over Autism,* by Catherine Maurice (1993).

The Autism Society of America defines autism as a treatable disorder (Sposato, 1995, p. 3). This means there are measures one can take which will make life somewhat better for a child with autism, and for his or her parents. However, treatable does not mean curable. As one prominent professional in the field of autism has said, "You better get used to it; you're in for the long haul" (Lovaas, 1991). Treatments are available, and they can make things better, but progress, when seen, can often be excruciatingly slow. It may take months or years for a child with autism to develop behaviors that parents just take for granted will emerge in children with normal development.

In general, the treatments available for individuals with autism

Fig. 7: Difficult and Slow Progress

usually fall into two categories: psychological/educational and pharmacological. There are some comprehensive programs, if you are fortunate enough to live near one, and if you are accepted into the program, and if you can afford it (Some programs are very expensive).

A program claiming one of the highest success rates is at the University of California in Los Angeles, and is headed by Ivar Lovaas. This program uses intensive behavioral modification beginning early in life. In one study, 47% of high-functioning children with autism treated in their intensive intervention program (40 hours per week of individual treatment, up to age 5) achieved normal functioning in two realms, the intellectual and the educational (Lovaas, 1987). Initially, Lovaas' program was touted as a cure, but later, in a letter to his colleagues, Lovaas stated: "The study does not use the word 'cure,' which would imply a removal of the presumably organic basis for autistic behavior" (Lovaas, 1990).

Another well-known program is the TEACCH (Treatment and Education of Autistic and Related Communication Handicapped Children and Adults) facility at the University of North Carolina in Chapel Hill. This is one of the most comprehensive programs, involving individual treatment plans, family involvement, and transitional services (Phelps & Grabowski, 1991).

Although any parents would be fortunate, relatively speaking, to have their child in one of these programs, there may be a cost to them, in terms of their personal freedom. To be most effective, the educational program of a child with autism must not stop at school, but continue over to the home. The ideal, for the child's development, would be a 24-hour program; this, however, is probably not ideal for most parents. Parents sometimes end up with a no-win choice: either leave things natural at home, and delay the child's development, as well as suffer the consequences of the child's behavior living in an unstructured environment; or, at the other extreme, thoroughly structure their home environment in response to the needs of the child, while sacrificing the needs of the other family members. The rights of the person with autism also need to be considered; he or she has, not only a legal right to habilitation, but also, arguably, a right to personal liberties, or, as one study put it, the right to "eat too many doughnuts and take a nap" (Bannerman, Sheldon, Sherman, & Harchik, 1990, pp. 80-81).

Most often, a child with autism is placed in a special education classroom in a regular school in the community, or, when possible,

Fig. 8: Parent's Dilemma

mainstreamed into a regular classroom, either with an aide or alone, depending on whether or not the child is disruptive to the rest of the class. Although most Special Education teachers are well-meaning, loving, and nurturing educators, they often have received little, if any, specialized training in working with children with autism. Unfortunately, education is a low priority, in terms of funding, in many areas of this country, and Special Education often receives only a little of the meager pie. As a result, most children with autism, who are among those in the greatest need of highly trained specialists to assess and treat them, may be educated by generalists. The children for whom this is not so are the ones whose parents become informed as to what is the best program, and then fight to get that for their child.

30   Living With Autism

One set of guidelines for educational program evaluation includes the following: early diagnosis and appropriate intervention; highly structured, skill-oriented teaching and treatment programs; data-based programs using individualized motivational systems tailored to specific individual needs; teaching areas that provide for intensive, distraction-free, one-on-one and small group sessions; and full-time, year-round instruction, from preschool through adulthood, involving multiple settings, including a comprehensive home-programming and parent-training program (Egel, 1989).

In addition, "All personnel involved with individuals with autism should be extensively, specifically trained and continuously evaluated. On-going skill-based staff training and evaluation are necessary to help ensure staff excellence" (Egel, 1989, p. 196). Ivar Lovaas and Tristram Smith (1994) believe that a six-month, full-time training period, with supervised one-on-one behavioral treatment, is necessary to adequately train service providers. In contrast, many educators receive their education on autism in one- or two-day workshops. "We estimate that the dissemination and practical use of what we now know about effective treatment [for autism] lies about 30 years behind what is currently known" (p. 258).

Often, parents will be left alone at home to do what they can with their child while they are not in school. What parents soon discover is that normal parenting skills often do not work with a child with autism. For example, children with autism may react to displays of parental disapproval quite differently than normal children would. They might, for example, smile or grin and exhibit the problem behavior more, rather than less.

Three manuals which can help parents cope with the day-to-day trials of living with autism are: Lorna Wing's *Autistic Child: A Guide for Parents and Professionals* (1985), Michael Powers' *Children with Autism: A Parent's Guide* (1989), and Ivar Lovaas' *The Me Book, Teaching Developmentally Disabled Children* (1981). Lorna Wing gives suggestions for managing such behaviors as screaming and temper tantrums, destructiveness, socially embarrassing behavior, resistance to change, eating problems, lack of fear of real dangers, odd movement and grimaces, and self-injury. Michael Powers outlines specific coping strategies to help families deal with the everyday stress of living with a special needs person, as well as giving information on national and local organizations serving individuals with autism. Ivar Lovaas outlines a step-by-step behavioral program to eliminate disruptive behaviors and add appropriate behaviors to a child's repertoire. But, as Lovaas (1991) says, "Be prepared for much hard work."

Fig. 9: Trying to Get Adequate Treatment

The parents of children with autism, like the parents of children with any chronic disorder, can be easy targets for claims of a miracle treatment. The latest alleged cure is an assisted communication program, called *facilitated communication*. Previously nonverbal, low-functioning individuals with autism have allegedly communicated, with this method, that they were really very intelligent and disliked having autism; some are even alleged to have communicated fluently in foreign languages (Seligman & Chideya, 1992). However, well-controlled, scientific studies have shown that the supposedly miraculous communication generated is typically the product of the facilitator (albeit unbeknownst to the facilitator), and not of the person with autism. In spite of this evidence, facilitated communication continues to have great appeal (Dillon, 1993; Mulick, Jacobson, & Kobe, 1993).

The major danger of using this technique is not only that it doesn't work, but that other, proven techniques are abandoned. Another problem is the occurrence of false allegations of abuse, sexual and otherwise. Fortunately, such allegations are dismissed by most courts. The only possible benefit is that the person with autism, who may have shown very little improvement in the past, and therefore received little reinforcement, may suddenly be seen as a cause celebre, and given much more attention. The problem, however, is that the reinforcement is meaningless, in that it is not contingent on any improvement in development. Until courts rule against those using this method (for not providing the best treatment available), this technique will, unfortunately, persist. A list of some other "miracle cures" for autism, all of which have met with disfavor over the years, can be found in *A Parent's Guide to Autism, Answers to the Most Common Questions,* by Charles Hart (1993).

Another major form of treatment is the use of medication. Medication, like education, can be used to treat, but not cure, autism. Some drugs, such as Thorazine or Haldol, may reduce some undesirable behaviors, such as temper tantrums and aggression, but they may also produce undesirable effects, such as seizures or tardive dyskinesia (facial grimacing or tongue protrusions). Other medications include Fenfluramine, vitamin B6-magnesium combinations, and tranquilizers. However, some of these have produced increased agitation in some individuals. A new, experimental drug for autism, Naltrexone, has shown some promise in reducing self-injurious behavior in studies both with animal models (Sahley & Panksepp, 1987) and with children with autism (Campbell, Anderson, Small, Lynch, & Choroco, 1990; Walters, Barrett, Feinstein, Mercurio, & Hole, 1990).

A report is available describing the drugs most commonly pre-scribed to children with autism, including appropriate dose ranges (Handen, 1993). Though parents may wish for a "magic bullet" cure for autism, certainly none is available now, nor does any seem to be in the near future, and the medications that are available may only serve to interfere, in the long run, with the educational improvement of the child with autism.

> At present, it seems possible that some children do respond positively to these treatments, while others respond negatively. Probably the majority of children have little response to them. In general, it is important to realize that educating, rather than medication, offers the best chance for improving problem behaviors in children with autism (Volkmar, 1989, p. 60).

One last educational issue involves the decision whether or not to educate the child about his or her autism. There is, to date, no empirical evidence collected on the consequences of this, but anec-dotal evidence, from both parents and high-functioning individuals with autism, indicates that telling children they have autism helps them to better understand themselves and their limitations in rela-tion to others (Akerley, 1988; ASA, 1990). This author is aware of only one book about autism written for children, entitled *Russell is Extra Special,* by Russell's father, Charles A. Amenta, III (1992).

Whether or not other people should be told a child is labelled autistic is another story. In one study, student teachers who were told a child was autistic gave more reinforcements for incorrect responses and less verbal correction than those who weren't told, which was, of course, potentially detrimental to the learning envi-ronment of the child with autism (Eikiseth & Lovaas, 1992).

Stresses on the Family

Some well-intentioned friends may say to parents, "At least your child is healthy," or, "At least your child is not retarded or mentally ill." But, as has already been mentioned, individuals with autism are often retarded, they have a mental illness caused by an organic deficit, and some may also have related health problems, such as seizures. In studies on the stress of parenting, the parents of children with autism, compared to the parents of children with any other type of handicap, are consistently the most stressed.

For example, one study compared the stresses of parenting children with a serious, chronic physical illness (cystic fibrosis, which results in physical incapacitation, the need for lifetime care, and eventually death), children with autism, and children with no physical or psychological disorder. The mothers of the children with autism scored significantly higher than all other mothers on the amount of overall stress experienced (Bourne & Schweitzer, 1990).

Parents of children with Down syndrome are frequently compared to the parents of children with autism. In one study, the Autistic Disorder sample of mothers had significantly lower perceived attachment and significantly lower gratification than the Down syndrome sample of mothers. For example, in response to the question, "Do you wish your child demonstrated more affection toward you?", 9 out of 10 mothers of children with Down syndrome said no, whereas 7 out of 10 mothers of children with autism said yes. To the question, "Does your child worry about or make an effort to win your approval?", 9 out of 10 mothers of children with Down syndrome answered yes, whereas only 3 of the autism group said yes. And when asked, "Do you ever feel like your child views you or treats you more like an object in his/her world?", all of the mothers of children with Down syndrome answered negatively, while 7 of the 10 mothers of children with autism answered positively (Hoppes & Harris, 1990).

Most of the studies of parental stress have been done with mothers, but one study did compare fathers of children with autism, children with Down syndrome, and children with normal development. In this study, the fathers of both groups of special needs children reported more problems than did the fathers of children with normal development, however, the fathers of children with autism differed in only a few areas from the fathers of children with Down syndrome. The authors suggest that, because mothers most often have primary responsibility for care of the children, the fathers may be more removed than their spouses from the most stressful day-to-day management activities (Rodrigue, Morgan, & Geffken, 1992).

Some studies have looked at specific behavioral problems and how they relate to the stress of parenting children with autism. The behavior that was found to be the best stress predictor was self-abusive behavior. The authors reported that the parents studied felt helpless, overwhelmed, and frightened by this disturbing, and often self-damaging, behavior. Hyperirritability and older age (of the children) were also major predictors of stress, especially for the mothers in the sample. Again it was felt that, since the mothers were usually more involved in the direct caregiving, they were more readily bothered by behaviors such as running out of the house or destroying objects. Also, managing these problems became more difficult for the mothers as their children got older and increased in size and strength (Konstantareas & Homatidis, 1989).

Another study found that the major differences between a sample of mothers of children with autism and a normative sample of mothers revolved around concerns for the child's future, especially after the parents were no longer able to provide for them. The mothers of children with autism were worried about their children's levels of cognitive impairment, their ability to function independently, and their ability to be accepted in the community (Koegel et al., 1992).

Parenting a child with autism can also take its toll on the marital relationship. Mothers of children with autism scored significantly lower on total intimacy than mothers of children with Down syndrome or mothers of children with average development, and also significantly lower on compatibility (spouses being able to work and play comfortably together). This second factor, the authors suggest, may be a reflection of the lack of recreation time available for each other and for the family because of the heavy burden of parenting, especially when respite care and other services are not available (Fisman & Wolf, 1991).

Fig. 10: Stresses on the Family

As well as taking a toll on the marital system, the presence of a child with autism seriously affects the family system as a whole. If there are siblings, the child with autism will undoubtedly receive a disproportionate share of the parents' attention. Also, because of the extreme difficulty in realizing even minimal gains in behavioral competence, this child will often receive much greater reinforcement for less absolute achievement. On occasion, young siblings who are not autistic have been known to start copying the behavior of their siblings who are. The lack of family recreational time mentioned above will also shortchange the siblings of children with autism. The siblings may be the target of negative autistic behaviors, ranging from indifference to aggressive threats and behaviors that threaten safety. They may also suffer social embarrassment over their sibling's condition. In addition, these siblings will have to consider that, someday, they too might have autistic children of their own.

A particularly poignant account of one such occurrence is *Without Reason, A Family Copes with Two Generations of Autism*, by Charles Hart (1989). When he is told of his son's diagnosis of autism, after being assured by his family doctor that there was no reason to believe his brother's autism was hereditary, Hart's despair is evident:

Looking at Ted in his immaculate suit, I thought of sparing him a torturous life of humiliation and failure by killing him. And yet my conscience could never bear that burden, even if it was to protect him from a grim future. A plan formed in my mind. We could take a ride on one of the state ferries. When the ship cruised into the deep waters of Puget Sound, I would hold my son close to me and jump overboard. Our suffering wouldn't last long and it would free Sara as a young widow so that she and Nick [his other son] could have a life that might approximate happiness (p. 53).

Other major stresses for the families of individuals with autism may include financial burdens (for specialized medical, psychological, speech, and respite care, for example), demands on the physical health and well-being of the parents, and housekeeping burdens. For example, one child was in the habit of smearing his feces all over his bedroom when he was locked in for the night to prevent him from roaming (DeMeyer & Goldberg, 1984).

Uncertain Long Range Forecast

One of the major anxieties of parents of children with autism is uncertainty about the future. Will their child get better or worse? What about sexuality? Will this become another major problem? Will they be able to be gainfully employed as adults? Will they ever be able to live independently? And if not, will the parents be able to manage them as adults? What about after the parents die; who will care for them?

To begin with, a child is considered independent when he or she reaches the age of 18, unless it is proven to a court that the person cannot be independent and is in need of a guardian for some or all of his or her affairs (Hart, 1993). Although this process goes smoothly for many parents, it can be a source of problems for others. The court appoints an independent attorney for the person with autism. This person may have very little, if any, knowledge of autism and may, for example, take the statements of a person with

Fig. 11: Uncertain Long Range Forecast

autism as factual. In one case, a very verbal 18-year-old boy told his attorney that he wanted to drive and live on his own and that his parents wouldn't let him. He also said that his parents had raped and abused him. The reality was that the boy was unable to safely cross a street by himself, let alone drive a car, and that he couldn't manage his own finances. For example, he often overpaid for services and then ran away before anyone could give him change. He also had no comprehension of the words rape and abuse. His parents, however, had to fight for the right to retain guardianship of their own child.

The adult needs of each individual with autism are very hard to predict. One method of doing so is to look at follow-up studies that examine a variety of outcomes and their likelihoods. Unfortunately, there are relatively few follow-up studies done on children with autism. Also, one might assume that a child today would have a better prognosis, given the improvements in education and treatment. One classic follow-up study by Leo Kanner originally appeared in 1971, and was reprinted in 1992. This study looked at 11 children with autism, three decades after they were originally reported on, in 1943. The results showed good news and bad news. Some had shown remarkable progress. For example, the progress of Donald T. is evident in a letter from his mother:

> Donald is now 36 years old, a bachelor living at home with us. . . . Since receiving his A.B. degree . . . he has worked in the local bank as a teller. . . . His chief hobby is golf, [which he plays] four or five times a week at the local country club. . . . Other interests are Kiwanis Club (served as President one term), Jaycees, Investment Club, Secretary of Presbyterian School. . . . Lack of initiative seems to be his most serious drawback. He takes very little part in social conversation and shows no interest in the opposite sex. . . . While Don is not completely normal, he has taken his place in society much better than we had ever hoped for (pp. 1-2).

Others did not fare nearly as well. Barbara was 37 years old and residing in a state hospital. Her ward physician wrote:

> She still has a stereotyped smile, the little girl-like facial expression with a placid grin, the child-like voice when uttering her parrot-like repetitions. Whenever I pass the ward, she greets me as follows: 'Doctor, do you know I socked you once?' . . . she shows a total absence of spontaneous sentence production; the same phrases are used over and over again with the same intonation. . . . she is childish, impulsive, subject to temper outbursts with stamping her feet, crying loudly and upsetting other patients (pp. 3-4).

This study, while showing the wide range of possible outcomes, reports the results of only a small sample and, therefore, provides no statistical data on the likelihood of the different outcomes. However, more recent studies, done in Japan, Canada,

England, and the United States, do provide statistics (Kobayashi, Murata, & Yoshinaga, 1992; Szatmari, Bartolucci, Bremner, Bond, & Rich, 1989; Venter, Lord, & Schopler, 1992).

Adolescence appears to be a critical time for development. In the Japanese study, almost half of a sample of 201 adults with autism (aged 18 or older) showed marked improvement during adolescence, while one third showed marked deterioration during that period of their lives.

In terms of employment, the Japanese study showed that 21% were gainfully employed. In another, smaller study, done in England and the United States and limited to high-functioning people with autism, 27% were gainfully employed. The Canadian study showed a 38% rate for gainful employment, but this study was done on very high-functioning people with autism (with an average IQ of 92). The jobs in the Japanese sample included bus conductor, laundry worker, auto mechanic, physical therapist, trash collector, cook, and dressmaker; those in the Canadian sample included salesman, librarian, physics tutor, and factory worker. The remaining subjects in all the studies worked in sheltered work-shops, were still in secondary school, or were unemployed.

A small number of subjects in the Japanese and British-American studies were attending or had graduated from a college, university, or advanced technical school. This figure was 5.5% in the Japanese study, and 4% (of subjects over 25 years old) in the British-American study. A remarkable 50% of the subjects in the Canadian study were in this group.

In terms of living arrangements, very few of the individuals studied lived on their own. There were none reported in the Japanese study, 2 out of 18 in the British-American study, and 5 out of 16 in the Canadian study. The remaining subjects lived at home with their parents, in a supervised home or apartment, or in a hospital.

None was married in either the Japanese or the British-American studies, and only one was married in the Canadian study. This finding is consistent with a study that specifically addressed the sexual knowledge and behavior of 11 male and 10 female high-functioning adolescents and adults with autism. The subjects of this study were obtained by contacting mental health care professionals, who were asked to recommend clients who functioned with some degree of independence and who could understand the content of the questionnaire. The average IQ of the male subjects was 84 and that of the females was 74, and both groups had a mean age of 27. Compared to a group of 10 males and 10 females of similar age with mental retardation and no autism, the autistic group showed significantly less sexual experience overall, even though they did not show significant differences in knowledge and interest. With the exception of masturbation (which 55% of the males with autism reported doing), sexual activity in the males with autism was very limited, with only 9% reporting that they had kissed a nonrelative of the opposite sex, and none reporting that they had "hugged or kissed for a long time" or that they had "gone further than hugging or kissing." Females with autism, although they reported less interest in sexuality and had a lower rate of masturbation (20%) than males with autism, reported that they had had more sexual experiences with others, with 20% saying that they had "hugged and kissed for a long time" and 10% saying they had "gone further than hugging and kissing." The conclusion was that people with autism probably have normal sexual drives and desires but do not have the social skills to have these materialize with another person (Ousley & Mesibov, 1991).

One study managed to locate 11 individuals (9 males and 2 females) with a mild form of autism who were married and were also parents (two of these parents were married to each other). They had a total of 44 children, 20 of whom were diagnosed as having autism. Six of the 11 appeared to be gainfully employed, while the remainder worked only intermittently or were on welfare. All continued to exhibit autistic behavior such as biting oneself, flapping arms, lining up objects, talking in monologues, or being socially isolated and inappropriate (Ritvo, Brothers, Freeman, & Pingree, 1988).

Although no study mentions anyone who was cured of autism, the Canadian follow-up study did find that 4 of the 16 high functioning subjects would be judged to be essentially normal by someone who did not know their history (Szatmari et al., 1989). Similarly, 8 of the 19 children in the original Lovaas study, when examined 6 years later, were judged to be indistinguishable from average children in two areas, intelligence and adaptive function

(McEachin, Smith, & Lovaas, 1993). The prospect, albeit remote, that a child with autism could ever be judged normal offers hope to parents. It can also be the source of parental frustration and guilt, if the child is not one of the fortunate few to develop in this way (Post, 1993). The reality is that most adults with autism today are not married, gainfully employed, or living independently.

Social Stigma

One of the major buffers against stress of any type is social support. Social support can take the form of information and/or advice, assistance with finances and services, acceptance from others, or companionship. Many studies have demonstrated that having social support systems is related to better psychological and mental health (Janoff-Bulman, 1992).

It would follow, then, that those under great stress, such as parents of children with autism, would be most in need of, and profit most from, strong support networks. Yet, rather than receiving this support, parents and their autistic offspring can be shunned, blamed, and stigmatized by society.

The presence of someone odd, different, or deviant makes many people, at best, uncomfortable and, at worst, outrightly hostile. A T-shirt sighted at a park in Pennsylvania reads: "I'd rather be dead than special." This same sentiment is echoed in a magazine article in which a person who voluntarily sits on the boards of three organizations working on behalf of the handicapped argues for the humane euthanasia of a man, named Henry, whose description strongly suggests he is an individual with autism (Lyle, 1992). Fortunately, most stigmatizing is not that blatant or cruel.

When children with autism are young, they often look and act like normal children whose parents are either neglecting or not controlling them. Children with autism don't have any distinctive physical features, as children with Down syndrome do, for example. In the case of autism, social stigma comes from ignorance; it ranges from stares and hostile glances to calls to social service agencies reporting physical abuse (of a child who won't stop crying or who has bruises from self-injurious behavior). Many parents say it would be easier on them if their child had some obvious

Fig. 12: Social Stigma

physical marker. Others have even considered putting a sign on their child (saying he or she has special needs) or having informational cards ready to distribute to people with critical stares or accusations.

As individuals with autism get older, their unusual behavior often stands out more, and they, rather than their parents, are more likely to be the targets of stigmatizing behavior. Fortunately, many adolescents and adults with autism seem to be oblivious to subtle social ostracism. Unfortunately, some people are so disturbed by individuals who are mentally different that they respond with more obvious snubs, such as name-calling, making mocking gestures, taunting and teasing, or even harming the person with autism.

Though strangers often cannot or will not provide social support, and may add more stress to parents already stressed to the maximum, at least one might hope that the immediate family would be helpful, and close families do often try to help. The most helpful support comes from those who can listen without blaming or accusing, who can empathize rather than minimize the difficulties, and who can show concern rather than criticism. The greatest gift to parents of autistic children is an offer of respite, a time in which they can be away from their children. Even well-intentioned grandparents and relatives, however, may be unable to manage a child with autism well enough to give respite to the weary parents, or the parents may feel it is too much to ask, even of a relative.

Some parents are fortunate enough to have respite services provided by a social service agency, especially if the agency screens its employees. Again, the challenge is to find a good respite worker, who is specifically trained in autism, who knows generally what to expect, and, ideally, who is trained to cope with this particular child. When a person with autism is left with a respite worker for days rather than hours (as in the case of a family wanting a vacation), the person's behavior may regress during the family's absence, and many parents feel that hard-won gains in behavioral improvement are not worth losing for a vacation.

Surviving and Transcending

Although living with a person with autism can be extremely trying, some people possess or develop strategies for coping with it. One of the most basic is simple habituating or becoming accustomed to their behaviors: After a period of time, the abnormal becomes the norm, which makes it easier to overlook. Charles Hart (1989) describes this phenomenon during a summer vacation at the beach with his family and his son's godfather, as well as the godfather's wife and two sons:

> "I had no idea of what you have to live with," Ted's
> godfather said after two days. Caught off guard by
> his comment, I asked him what he meant. "I don't
> know how your family can live like that," he went
> on, listing the many compromises and accommoda-

tions to which we had grown accustomed. It came as a shock to hear an old friend speak so honestly about Ted. Sara and I had spent so many years trying to focus on the positive side, no matter how small, celebrating each sign of progress, that we had lost our sense of perspective. We had overlooked the extensive damage to our family life, the price paid by Nick as well as ourselves (p. 167).

Fig. 13: Surviving and Transcending

In a study on the mothers of individuals with autism, the best predictor of coping was a personality variable called hardiness. Hardiness reflects the extent to which a person feels in control of the environment, sees meaning in life, and feels challenged by problems (Gill & Harris, 1991).

In a similar study, mothers of mentally retarded children who felt in control and/or were religious, as defined by traditional religious practice (e.g., attendance at church, belief in a God), were better able to cope with their situation (Friedrich, Cohen, & Wilturner, 1988).

Living with someone with autism is never boring. The person's thinking, logic, and behavior is strange, often enigmatic, and one may be drawn into a never-ending quest to see the world from the autistic perspective. Sometimes one is successful, and most of the time one is not; but the success, because it is so rare and comes after such a struggle, can be very precious and satisfying.

> Anything they do can . . . move us, thrill us, reduce us to tears. On more than one occasion, I have made a fool out of myself by clutching a near-stranger's arm and rhapsodizing about my children. "Oh my God, look at Michel! . . . What beautiful playing with the other children!" As she politely, though with some perplexity, agrees, I tell myself to cool it a little; I'm trying to remember what "normal" is supposed to mean in a mother (Maurice, 1993, pp. 295-296).

The behavior of a person with autism, especially the social behavior, can also be viewed from a comic perspective. At one conference (ASA, 1991), parents were invited to share funny stories. Some stories were about the children's lack of awareness of what was happening to their own bodies. One boy with autism lost one of his baby teeth during breakfast. As it fell out of his mouth and onto his pancakes, he angrily queried, "Who put this tooth on my pancakes?" Others were about lack of awareness of social graces. One boy, cutting into a formal line to shake a Bishop's hand, said, "French toast." Another girl, visiting her pillar-of-dignity great aunt, asked, "Where's the god-damned bathroom?" Other examples reflect misunderstandings. One boy, when asked what date it was, read the calendar literally and said, "Today is Dec. 24th and 31st, 1990." An article from *The Advocate* (Dillon,

1988) lists amusing neologisms created by one boy with autism. For example, he coined the word *birdilizer* after he watched his father bury a bird that had died while flying into a window.

Fig. 14: Literal Interpretation

Parents of individuals with autism often talk about how having a child with autism has helped them find the strength to develop the assertiveness they needed to get educational institutions and social service agencies to meet their child's needs. Some parents have become social advocates and leaders in local and national autism societies. Other parents (and siblings) have developed their careers around the issues of the handicapped and have become, for example, lawyers defending the rights of the handicapped or college professors educating others about the needs of the mentally ill.

Harold Kushner, in his best selling book, *When Bad Things Happen to Good People* (1983), writes about his own tragic and triumphant experience with his son, who suffered from a rare and fatal degenerative disease. "I am a more sensitive person, a more effective pastor, a more sympathetic counselor because of Aaron's life and death than I would have been without it" (p. 133). However, he goes on to add:

> And I would give up all those gains in a second if I
> could have my son back. If I could choose, I would
> forego all the spiritual growth and depth which has
> come my way, because of our experience, and be

what I was 15 years ago, an average rabbi, an indifferent counselor, helping some people and unable to
help others, and be the father of a bright, happy boy.
But I cannot choose (pp. 133-134)

The same is true of parents of children with autism. They are
in a constant battle with this disorder called autism, which they
have not chosen to fight. And, although few, if any, would choose
to repeat the battle, they often gain great wisdom from their experiences.

Chapter 2
The Ballerina

This is the story of a little 7-year-old girl Jenny, as told by her mother, Karen. Jenny lives with her mother and father and her 5-year-old sister. Her mother has made the decision to stay at home with her children while her father works for a local manufacturing company. The interview took place in their home while the two girls were away at school.

Diagnosis

[I first suspected that something was wrong with Jenny when] she was about 18 months old. It's usually the time they start putting two words together, like up please, more juice, bye bye, and she wasn't really even using one word. It was her lack of speech and the temper. She would throw wicked fits that would last a half hour to 2 hours or 2½. Sometimes they just seemed to go on forever. She'd throw herself onto the floor and stay there and scream like somebody was beating on her—[like] somebody invisible was there abusing her. [She would] thrash her arms and legs around like crazy, and she would just scream, scream, scream, and nothing I did would do any good. I would just let her scream. I would pull her onto the carpeted area so she wouldn't give herself a concussion and just let her scream. There was nothing I could do to stop her.

It was just for no reason. It wasn't like I would tell her no and she would get angry. I would just walk into a room and there she would be on the floor pitching a fit. [She did this from the time she was] 18 months to about 3½, several times a week and at night when she was in her room. She wouldn't sleep; she'd be screaming all night long, crying, crying. She seemed never to need sleep.

I spoke to our pediatrician and he said that, as quickly as I could without running, [I should] get up and leave the room so she wouldn't have my attention, and I tried that and it didn't work. I kept calling him up, telling him I'm going to kill her, I can't handle this any longer. She's screaming, she's driving me nuts, I don't know what to do. He [said] she was seeking attention. She was throwing a fit to get my attention. If I didn't protect [her] she would have hurt herself, so I had to be around when she was doing it to make sure she wasn't going to bang her head on the floor or on a piece of furniture.

When I told him she wasn't verbalizing very much, he told me [that] children develop at different stages. "She's not really behind. Just wait it out." She was my first child and I was young, and I think that was what the doctors were thinking. My pediatrician ignored all my concerns [about her size], because she was very tiny and fragile. I think he probably just felt I was ignorant of child-rearing, but I'd been around children, and I'd read every book I could get my hands on when I was pregnant.

I knew something was not right, but I did not want to believe it, and everybody kept telling me that everything is okay. And I wanted to believe that, even though, my God, everything was not okay. So I was tormented between my own feelings of knowing something was wrong and wanting to believe everybody. I talked to friends and strangers, anybody who would listen to me, and they would say, you're comparing your child to other children. One person told me that all I wanted was a genius, and all I wanted was an average child. I just wanted a very average, normal little girl. A normal little girl I could do things with.

I couldn't do anything with her except nurse her when she was little; that was the only real contact she gave me. She would mold into my body and suckle for hours. She loved it and it was such a good bond, but when my husband would try to pick her up, she would become stiff; she wouldn't let him hold her. She would squirm and kind of whine and really stiffen like a board. He'd say, "She doesn't love me," and I'd say, "Of course she loves you. She's your baby." But I saw that happening and it was strange. I'd always seen children wanting to be held, needing to be touched to the point where you'd say, "Go away! You're bothering me." Except she wasn't like that.

Labelling

I was pregnant with my second child, eight or nine months pregnant, and I finally went into [my pediatrician's] office and said, "Something has to be done. I cannot take this anymore. I'm having another baby. I can't deal with it. What am I going to do with a little baby when this one screams constantly?" And that's when he said, "Okay. Her speech is a little behind, but she's still in the norm." He was still denying there were any problems. She's three years old and she has maybe one word answers, so he recommended speech therapy. [The clinic] recommended me to a psychologist, [and Jen] was referred to a school where they had a toddler class for special needs children.

[The first person to use the word autistic was the director of her toddler group. She] came to make a home visit. I think Jen was 3½ or 3, and she came to my house, and she followed her and watched what she was up to. And she said, "Karen, you know Jenny looks as though she may have some autistic characteristics." And I must have turned sheet white, because she grabbed my shoulder and she said, "I'm not saying she's autistic or anything. I'm just saying she has some of the characteristics." She was the first person, until a couple of years later, that actually went out on a limb and said, this is what it might be. Nobody wants to put a label on a child, in case they're wrong or for whatever reason. They don't want to say this child's retarded, this child is developmentally delayed, or whatever. She was the first person who actually told me what she was thinking.

My stomach kind of flip-flopped when I first heard her teacher tell me that she looked as though she had some of those characteristics, because I [had seen] a show where a boy from St. Elsewhere was being violent and striking out, lashing out, being nonverbal, being severely handicapped, and that scared me.

[I went back to the pediatrician] and then finally we had a CAT scan done. She had [had] a sweat test done when she was a toddler because she was very small. She was slow gaining weight. She was very tiny, very fragile looking. That came back negative. He didn't tell me what the condition was that she might have had, just [that] it wasn't bad. So finally, my husband and I saw a psychologist. He observed Jenny; she was 4 years and 1 month. I'll never forget—he told me I needed help. He did finally put down on paper she had a developmentally delayed personality and she looked as though she was autistic-like, but he also told me that I needed counseling. I needed to have some sort of talk to someone on how to raise this child. When you have children, you don't know what to do anyway, and with a special needs child you really don't know what to do. So I came out of his office kind of great and bad. Finally, we have a label, so we can go from there, and I can do whatever I have to do for her, and then, on the other hand, I felt really badly, because he told me, I kind of had the feeling, that I wasn't good enough. I wasn't doing my job as a mother; I needed help. It wasn't just her that had a problem; it was me. And I was a little annoyed, because everything I have learned that works with my daughter, I have learned from her. She has taught me what works. She needs to be handled very firmly, to know what's expected of her. Rules can't change, they have to be the same, and she responds to discipline and love. She really responds very well. I came out of his office thinking, hey I have a problem too; now what do I do? So I just said, okay, whatever he said, fine, and it just went in one ear and out the other. When I mulled it over, [I thought], at least I have a diagnosis, and we can use it for insurance companies or schooling or whatever educational program she might need, since I wanted her in a certain placement, and finally I have what she needs. The question was finally answered [as to] what is going on here.

Cause

It wasn't that you could say this happened during my pregnancy. I was the healthiest pregnant woman alive. I wasn't smoking while I was pregnant. I ate lasagna once a week for nine months, practically. I craved good food, I drank enough milk for a whole slew of children, and I felt wonderful. You know, I never had morning sickness; I had lots of energy. I went hiking, swimming, biking, all those things. I felt great.

It was nineteen hours from the time my water broke to the time I had her. It wasn't all hard labor. There was some time after my water broke, so my contractions varied. [During the delivery,] she had a monitor put on her scalp, because they couldn't find her heartbeat after a while. And I had an epidural, and she was a posterior, so he used forceps. And when they turned her, she really wasn't very cooperative, and they had to turn her again. And she had some red marks on her face, but there was no tearing of the skin or anything. It may or may not have caused it. I don't think that was it. I just think it was fate, the way she was supposed to be.

I always thought babies came out screaming their heads off. When she came out, she was very quiet. I didn't even know she was there. Where's my baby, where's my baby? Not a peep out of her, for a couple minutes. It was very strange.

Grief and Sorrow

[My husband] was very strong [when he heard]; he was too strong. I'm the one who cried and cried and cried. I'm the one who blamed everybody or [convinced] myself that something happened when she was delivered. The obstetrician had to have done something, because I had a picture perfect pregnancy. It had to be somebody's fault. I looked around for somebody to blame. During all that time, I cried and cried. My husband was there for me. He was very supportive. He was very strong. He took his own feelings and put them on the shelf and he tended to me. He held me, he talked to me, he told me it wasn't my fault, these things happen, we're going to be okay, we'll deal with this, we have a good marriage. But by doing that, he neglected his own feelings. So when I finally became okay and was able to accept things the way they were and go on from there, I realized he'd never dealt with his own feelings, so they were still inside him, buried. So whenever he talked about her future, especially if somebody would say something to him about our daughter, he would start to cry. But he wouldn't show it. You know how men are, they can't show their feelings. So he would hold it in, and he would feel really bad. I know it's because he was there [for me] for those two years that I cried and cried. He helped me so much, for me to be okay, that he didn't help himself. He helped me too much. Instead of crying together, he was my rock. He kept me going, always reassured me that we would make it, and by doing that, he denied his own feelings, and then they became very overwhelming for him.

It took a couple of years, when she was, like, 4 or 5 years old, and I would talk to him about it, and say, okay, I'm finally starting to be all right, I'm not going to cry anymore, because it's no good for me and not good for my husband and for my babies. And he just couldn't talk about it without getting teary-eyed. So it was my turn to help him. Instead of healing our wound together, we did it separately. It took a while, but we did not know how else to do it. We were going by what our emotions told us to do. He felt he had to be strong for me, and I felt I had to cry and blame everybody I could think of, but by doing that, I got it out. I cried so much I couldn't cry any more, and then I realized, I'm not helping anybody by doing this, and finally I got all these feelings out.

The little girl I thought I had was lost. [She] was this new, unique little person, who was almost like a stranger to me. I had to mother her and bond all over again in a different way. So I looked at her in one light, and then all of a sudden she was different; it was not the child I thought I had. And that was a hard realization. For years, I thought I had this little girl who was a little behind, but she'd catch up. [That's what I was told] and that's what I wanted to believe. I was told Einstein did not talk until he was five, and all these things people told me, and I knew something was amiss, but I wanted to believe these people.

Day-to-Day Living

[Her behavior today is different from that of other children. For example,] what she wears to bed is very unusual for a $7\frac{1}{2}$-year-old. We put a diaper on her at night, because she is incontinent at night. Without a diaper, she'll smear her feces and have a free-for-all in her room. That's been going on, off and on, since she was about 3. When she was younger, it would be anywhere and everywhere, her face, her mouth, up her nose. She would have it all over the floor, the walls, and her bed. Now the rare times she does it, she usually keeps it in her bed, on her person, and on her bedclothes. So we make sure she has a diaper every night, so she doesn't do that.

Over her jammie pants we put on a pair of cut-off jean shorts, and we put a belt through the loops, and we latch it in the back, so she cannot take off her shorts and her diaper, so she cannot pee in her bed. That's a little unusual, like a chastity belt, sort of. You have to be very inventive, trying to figure something out, and what else can you do? You have to keep the diaper on, and it is very easy to take the diaper off.

She was almost five before she would consistently sleep through the night, and I thought I was going to die of exhaustion. It's amazing to see how little sleep you can live on when you really have to. And I had to. When she was younger, we lived in a different apartment, and her room was adjacent to ours. She would scream and there was nothing we could do, put pillows over our heads. She wouldn't stop. There were nights she didn't sleep at all. And neither did I.

She would take off all her clothes (before we got diapers for her), take all her clothes, winter clothes, summer clothes, out of all her drawers, put them in her bed, and try on clothes all night long. And she would wet her bed, and the next morning I'd have five loads of laundry to do. She'd wet all over all of her clothes. So, little by little, her room emptied out. We took out her bureau, her toy box; I took out her little table, her chairs. Eventually, all she had was her bed, and that was it. Anything [we left] in there she would just use to keep herself awake. The night was long for her. It was long for me.

Little by little, we tried it again, and now she leaves (*Karen knocks on wood*) everything alone. She leaves her drawers alone for the most part, or sometimes she'll take out a sweater or two and try them on, but she doesn't go crazy in there any more, with all her clothes. And sometimes she's half naked in the morning when I go in (she loves to be without clothes), but she's okay. That's fine, that little bit of a mess I can deal with.

I usually put out her clothes the night before. She can dress herself, but she has a hard time snapping. She likes over-sized clothes—big tee-shirts, big sweat shirts. She puts her hands inside the sleeves, and the sleeves are hanging over her fingers, and she flaps them in front of her face. She flaps her arms like she's flying. She must get the breeze and feel cozy inside, because she snuggles herself up, like she's hugging herself, and she just seems very content.

She knows how to brush her teeth, but she doesn't like to. I usually do it first and have her do some part of it when I'm done.

And she toilets herself. She's into privacy lately, so I can't go in to make sure she's not going to smear. She slams the door in my face, but that's normal for 7-year-olds to want. But she won't wipe unless I give her a tissue. "Here. Wipe your vagina now." And then she will. [She doesn't ask to be wiped,] so you just have to be aware. I just have to catch it. Usually I don't catch her in time.

[She has certain favorite foods she likes to eat.] She lives on Cream of Wheat, peanut butter, and cheese. She craves those foods. When she was younger, she would eat Kix for two months, and nothing else. And then she would eat Cheerios and nothing else. She's basically a vegetarian. I can't get too much meat into her, unless it's [those frozen] salisbury steaks that you can taste forever? She likes those a lot! They're fatty, they're really not that nutritious, but it's the only protein, other than peanut butter, I can get into her.

She likes to pour her juice. I have a little Tupperware container that's a really good size for her. And she likes to watch it fill up and then pour over. I have to watch she doesn't pour the whole jug. She likes the motion, and she sort of gets mesmerized by the whole thing. I think it's not so much that she doesn't understand, I think she knows exactly what she's doing, but she likes to see it fill up and then pour over.

When she gets really antsy and bored, like on a school vacation, she tends to eat constantly. A lot of women do, when they're not happy or bored. So I think it's very typical of a little female, [but] she won't stop. And then, if I tell her no, she'll get really angry. She'll whine a little bit, or cry a little bit, and go bounce herself against the couch when she's angry. So I'll put on some kiddie music or something, and she'll go bounce on my bed. That calms her down, and she enjoys it. She kind of dances to it.

It doesn't have to be kiddie music. Lots of times she'll push the button on my stereo, the music will come on, and she'll go bouncing on my bed. And she's, like, in a music world of her own, and she's very happy, and it's appropriate. So everything that she does that's appropriate for her age, I try to encourage, even though I'm taking a chance by doing that. Like, if she's going to the bathroom on her own, and she doesn't want me to go in. There's a chance she's going to have a big mess all over the toilet seat when I go in there. But it's very typical of a 7-year-old. So I tell her, it's all right, you want privacy, but if you need me, call me, even though I know she won't. So I [just] pray she doesn't go in the bathroom and have a free-for-all. Most times she doesn't, so I take that chance, but I'm trying to encourage something that is more important.

[There are different things she does during the day to occupy herself. Her favorite toy is] a Beetlejuice [doll]. He's real ugly, but there's something about it. She carries it around for hours. His head comes off, and he's got this snake head underneath. He's got a Beetlejuice head that goes on top of it, and there's a button in back that makes his head go up and down. She likes that an awful lot. She likes her blocks, and she likes her books. She loves Playdoh; she eats it. She likes to smash it, and if she sees that you're not looking (she's very sneaky, there's a lot going on up there, she knows an awful lot), if she sees that you're turned away, she'll rub it across her lips, and I know she's getting the salt across her lips. [She knows] not to put it in her mouth, because I'll be mad at her. I get on her about eating Playdoh, even though I know it's nontoxic; it's just not appropriate.

She figures things out, and she giggles, like, I'm playing a game on you. Like you'll say, "Come here, get dressed," and she'll take off the other way and laugh hysterically. She knows exactly what she's doing, and she gets off on it. She loves water. She loves dirt. She used to eat it. She likes contact, stuff on her.

This Christmas was a lot of fun. She participated. She really got into unwrapping presents. It's not the idea of looking to see what's inside it, it's the idea of unwrapping—the sound, something, I don't know.

Every year, what to get her is a dilemma, because I don't always want to get her baby toys, but that's what she likes. They have mirrors and make sounds, you know, they have a rattle inside of them. I feel like I should not be buying infant toys for a 7-year-old. A 7-year-old should not be wearing a diaper. A 7-year-old should not be doing this or that or the other thing. And I try to make her as much age appropriate as I can, but, every Christmas, I find myself going down the baby aisle for the little cute rattles that play music. And it bothers me every Christmas. The only time I let autism really affect me is in December, every December. I weep a little bit. I see Santa and all the little kids and my youngest daughter on Santa's lap, and she says, "I want this Barbie, and I want that Ken, and I want all these things." And I look at my daughter, Jenny, and she can't do that. She can't tell what she wants. She'd take off his beard and his hat. It would be a fiasco. I get depressed, even though I love the holidays. It's kids, it's fun. It's a very happy time of the year. This year, at least, she appreciated the wrappings and stuff. I think that had a lot to do with it, because she participated more than in Decembers gone by. It made that little depression I get every December a little bit easier to handle.

She's very physical. She can climb. She can run, like a lightening bolt, very strong, very quick. And when she sees you with a glass of ice water, before you can say, "Jenny, no!" she's got the ice out of the glass. Like a little Kung Fu person. It's like a contradiction, because it seems, at times, that she is clumsy. Like the way she walks, she'll lean on stuff. I'll say, "Stand up straight, you're bugging me," you know, getting on my nerves. She doesn't really trip over things or fall into stuff, like she used to when she was younger. She would run and hit her arms in the doorways, like she didn't know where they were in relation to her body. And now she almost never gets hurt. She's very physical; she climbs like a monkey.

[She does have problems with her speech, however.] She can repeat almost anything. It doesn't sound very clear, and if you didn't know what she was saying, you probably wouldn't recognize it. So she can say almost anything, but spontaneously, especially appropriately and spontaneously, there's very few things. She will say, "shirt," as I'm getting her dressed, and I'll say, "That's right, we're putting on a shirt." But if I say, "We're putting on your sh—," she may or may not say, "shirt," but a lot of times she won't. She will say Mommy and Daddy on occasion. Out of the blue, like if my husband is playing with her: "Daddy!" She almost seems to sing a lot of the words she's saying.

[If she wants you,] she'll grab you, or she'll take you by the head, and push you out of the chair, or she'll kiss you. That's her way of letting you know she really wants something. She'll give you her cheek, cause she very rarely kisses on the mouth. She will give you her cheek: "Kiss me, I want something." I used to use that, you know: you want that cookie, give Mommy a kiss, and I'll give you this cookie. You know, because she never gave me any love. And I was dying for hugs, my heart was breaking, my arms were aching for her to hug me. So if she wanted something, I'd say, "Give Mommy a kiss." It's mean, but I wanted a hug so bad. I had to really struggle to get that hug, but I got it. I would invade her space all the time, and she would get really ticked off at me, but I would grab her, and I would say, "I'm coming in! You won't come out, I'm coming in to get you. And you can scream and cry all you want." And she did. But I'm coming in to get you if you're not coming out. I'm going to invade your space, I'm going to make you mad, I'm going to keep doing this, over and over and over again, until you allow me to come into your world, if you won't come out into mine. And I made her mad a lot.

But now she'll hug, she'll kiss, she'll play, she'll interact, especially with adults. She loves to interact with adults. [When] I have friends come over, she'll ask them to get her something to eat, if I've said no. She'll get my friend, Diane, and push her off the couch, like, I'll get this one! She knows she's easy. And my sister-in-law, she knows she's easy too. So if I said no about something, she'll bypass me and go all the way around and get my sister-in-law. And she'll say, "Pushes," which is her magic word that means, I want something, help me. So my sister-in-law will go in the pantry with her and say, "Oh, Karen, can she have this?"

She's very independent. [For me] it's like give and take. Do I want her to be independent or do I want to fight to get verbal language from her? If she wants that Cream of Wheat, then I say, "If you want it, you have to talk to me. What do you want, Cream?" And she'll say, "Cream of Wheat." Good, I'm making her talk. But if I leave it in the pantry where she can climb and get it herself, she'll get the packet, she'll get the bowl, she'll get the spoon, she'll put it all on the table, and by doing that, she's very independent, doing for herself. What do I want? Which is more important? I think the independence is more important. If you never speak, ever at all in your life, and you can take care of yourself, that's more important.

She will [also] make eye contact now, complete eye contact. When she was younger, she wouldn't look you in the eye; it was as though she was feeling pain as she looked at you. Now she'll get right in your face and touch you, get nose to nose with you. And that's a far cry from where she was before.

[But] she's less sensitive to pain. My mother has radiators in her house, and she can sit on one for a couple of seconds before she has to get off, and I can just barely touch it and it hurts me. And sometimes she falls down like a ton of bricks, and she might get up and cry from the anger of falling, but not because she's hurt. When she was little, she would fall down face first and get up and just keep on running.

When she started walking, she ran. She runs on her toes, like a little ballerina. She just hops, like she's got springs on her ankles. I almost never see her walk. She jumps, jumps in place. It's very annoying. You live with a person who never sits still and, after a while, you don't really realize how nervous you are, until you go, hey, I'm nervous, so you better stop that. Because you're so used to it, you don't even know that you're nervous. It's like living with a little Mexican jumping bean, something that never ever sits still.

[Also,] she's very affectionate now with my husband and myself. She loves my father [too], he's kind of like her father. My husband is like a big plaything. She's very happy when she's around him. She likes my mother, you know how grammies are. She knows [that] when she goes to my mother's house, she's going to be spoiled a lot. She loves women more than men, unless she knows that male very, very well. Her new aide at school is a man, and she's taken to him right away. That's very unusual. He has a beard, just like my husband. He's very soft-spoken, very sweet, a very nice guy. There's no woman I know of that she's afraid of, or that she doesn't really like to be around. Unless this person's looking in her mouth or something. Then that's a different story. Like the hygienist: she does not like the hygienist. But any other woman she feels very comfortable being around.

She's a very, very happy girl for the most part; she's happy almost always. Sometimes she will giggle rather than cry, but that has gotten better. She's getting more appropriate emotions for situations. A lot of her has calmed down. She still needs to bounce, but I put an ugly rocking chair here, and every morning before school she'll rock in it, and that's more appropriate than flinging herself against furniture.

When she's around glass, I have to be careful, because she has a glass fetish. She likes windows and glass storm doors. When we go to K-Mart, she licks the glass doors going in. It makes my stomach queasy, you know, [you just] don't do that. I remember my mother saying, "You don't know who touched that or what they had."

She [broke] her bedroom window the first ice storm we had. I had contact paper on it, because she used to bang her head and her palms into the window, so I put contact paper over it, so she couldn't see [that it was a window]. At the time, she was really into flowers, so I picked out flowers contact paper. I heard her in her room. She was saying, "Flower, flower . . ." I'm like, okay, there has to be a flower in there somewhere, or she wouldn't be saying *flower*. [So I went into her room,] and she was feeling the wallpaper all the way up, saying, "Flower . . . ," [and the window was broken]. I should have had teddy bears or something, so she wouldn't have been intrigued, and that would have been the end of it. But [it's a good thing I put something on it, because] if it wasn't for the contact paper being on that window, it would have shattered.

Masturbation was [also] a big [problem] for a little while. Especially in the bathtub. She loves to be naked, she's always loved to be naked. I do too. It feels nice not to have anything constricting on, you know. If she didn't smear or wet her bed, I would let her sleep naked or just little underwear on or something. But when masturbation came about, I said no, it's too much. She would put toys into her panties, and when the girls would be getting ready to have a bath, she'd get in and she would straddle the stream of water. My girl's very inventive. So how do I stop something that must feel really good to her? I just make sure she has something to do. I get her dressed right away, and she wears a dress to school, and she wears tights. She's never with just a dress and panties. She has something else on, just so she can't get to it. With panties, you can get in there very easily if you wanted to.

We have one cat, Sneaky, who will be 12 years old this summer, so he's always been here. She's always known him, and she loves him. And it's a good thing he's very tolerant, and so is my other cat, because she's not always very gentle, although she doesn't go out of her way to hurt them. She just loves too much; she'll squeeze too hard. She's never actually been mean to them on purpose. She's never really been that aggressive toward other people, but she did hit herself on the nose a lot when she had the flu and she couldn't breathe. She'd get angry, and she'd smack herself. When she gets angry, she'll smack the side of her head, but never to the point where she'd leave a bruise or anything.

[What troubles me most about Jenny] is what she's forgotten. When she was 2, she knew animal sounds. That's when she peaked with her speech, at 2, and then it dropped off. She lost some stuff that she had. We would ask her, "What does the monkey say? What does the dog say? What does the cat say. What does the bird say?" We'd ask her twenty different animals, and she would answer the questions. And then that disappeared. From what I've heard, it's supposed to be easier for them to relearn something that they've lost than it is for them to learn something new. [But] she never really relearned any of those things. Once it was gone, it was gone. So now I worry that she might forget something basic, like going to the bathroom, or sleeping, and then have that be totally gone and never come back too.

Treatment

We've found out she's a lot more intelligent than we ever gave her credit for. We're doing what's called facilitated communication at school, and she's been doing fantastic with it. Absolutely out of this world, typing out sentences, and at home I can get yes or no or what's in front of her. Like, if you want hot chocolate, spell it! I can get her to do that. But if it's something I don't know the answer to, I don't get the answer. I mean she's not comfortable with me, I'm not the teacher. If I ask, "What did you have to eat at school?"—-I don't know what she had—-it's hard to get that out [of her]. [But if I ask, "Do you want hot chocolate?",] I can get *yes* or *no*. I have to say, "If you want this, type it out, and I will give it to you." And she'll type out *hot chocolate*, and she'll spell it correctly. I used to hold her fingers down to the pointer, and now I just hold my two fingers under her wrist and she points herself. She has her hand [on the pointer], and I put two fingers on her wrist, and I draw her back after each point, and she does really well.

It's still new for her; she's been doing it a little less than a year. I have the little paper I keep by the microwave in the kitchen, so when she wants something to eat, I make her work for it. I let her off in the morning, because she doesn't have the patience, and I don't either. So breakfast is free.

She does really well at school, especially for her teacher, Kristie. She does fantastic work with Kristie; I am amazed. Kristie calls me up and tells me what she's typed out, and it's as if they are talking about someone else's child. [One time,] I asked her to find out for me why she doesn't facilitate as well at home as she does at school, and she typed out *because my parents don't believe in me*. So it was quite a blow. I felt really badly. Around Christmas time, they were asking, "Do you like Christmas?", and she kept typing out *no*. And they kept saying, "Why? Do you like presents?" *Yes*. "Do you like Santa?" *Yes*. "What is it about Christmas you don't like?" *Money*. And during group, she stood up and shouted out, "Money!", and sat back down. And that was very unusual for her, to come out with words, especially that kind of a word. It's not like she came out with *juice* or something. This was something that is a concept, something she really doesn't have much to do with. And they asked her, "What is it about money you don't like?" And I had thought maybe she heard us talking that money was tight, we had to be careful this Christmas and watch our funds, or whatever. I was feeling bad [that] we were imposing our feelings on her, like she was a burden or something like that. But she typed out about money that she couldn't buy her parents anything. And I thought, wow. So Kristie asked her, "How about your mother gives you money and you go shopping?" And she adamantly typed *no*.

Kristie called me and said, "Well, how about you send me a few dollars, and I'll have Jenny do some chores around school, and she'll earn her money?" And then Kristie took her shopping to the dime store, and she picked out what was appropriate for us. I got a bracelet and a trinket box for jewelry and stuff, my husband got a coffee mug, and her sister got a coloring book. She had *yes* and *no* written on a piece of paper. When asked, "Do you want to get this for your mother?", [she pointed to] *no*. Everything was *no*. And Kristie finally said, "You have to do something. Do you want this?" *Yes*. And it wound up being very appropriate presents, and she earned her money, so it was her own. She didn't want to be given money.

I could not know that all this was going on inside of her. She's very, very smart. She's doing multiplication at school, she's telling time, and they asked her, "How did you know how to tell time?" And she typed out *I had to teach myself*. Cool. This is blowing my mind, you know. But I don't get that kind of thing at home, I don't get all these sentences.

[*The interviewer asked Karen the following additional questions to see if Jenny's behavior matched her ability as shown by facilitated communication, because the validity of this technique has been questioned, as was mentioned earlier. "Other than that facilitated communication message, does money, as far as you're concerned, mean anything to her, from your experience? If you put money out, for example, would she want it? Could you give her money for a present?"*] Not that I can tell. She likes to smell dollar bills. She likes to feel them, hold them across her face, her mouth, but she's never given me the impression that she wanted money. It could just as easily been a pen or a crayon. There's not a lot she's ever shown me that she wants, other than food and Playdoh.

They sign in class, [but] I don't think the signs mean a whole lot [to her]. She probably understands them when she sees them, but she doesn't do it herself. When she's upset, she'll make the sign for *more*, but I don't know if that's because she's upset or it's just something she's done on her own, or whatever. I know a few [signs] and I try using them, but she doesn't really seem to respond. I'd rather have verbal speech. If the signing would work, if she seemed really interested in it, then I would do more with that.

I don't always know how to reprimand her, so sometimes I just take her by the shoulders and tell her what she's done wrong and why I'm angry. Spanking won't work with her, so I'll yell at her and tell her, "Don't do that, that's boo boos, you will hurt yourself, you could kill yourself." If I'm yelling at her, that breaks her heart. So that works more than spanking would, because she doesn't always feel pain anyway. And then she'll cry, and then I want to hug her, I want to tell her, I'm sorry; Mommy's doing it for your own good. I have to walk away and tell myself I have to yell at her. I have to give her discipline, just like her sister needs discipline. You have to do something, so I just walk away, and I keep my emotions inside, but I think she probably knows how I feel.

[Sometimes, if she's done something bad, I do a time-out.] I put her on the couch, or I'll find a little place—between my bed and the wall there's a little space where she can sit in there and not be able to see anyone—so she sits on the floor by the bed and by the wall, that's maybe two feet wide. She likes to be contained in something anyway. [I tell her,] "Good-bye, you're having time-out." But she's so sneaky. If I leave for another room, she'll get up and sneak and sit on a chair, and sometimes she's so sneaky, I don't realize [it].

What feels right, I do. I've had a lot of people tell me, I shouldn't do this, I shouldn't do that, I should do this, I should do that: so many contradictory things from so many people. If I followed everybody's advice, my mind would be all completely confused, you know. I just can't do that. People who don't have an autistic child, they don't understand. I do what I think works. It's like, okay, what kind of a kid do I have today? Do I have a very happy, goofy kid that I can't get through to, or a little screaming meemie that I can't get through to, or do I have a very nice, mellow little girl (that's very rare) that I may or may not be able to get through to.

Someone told me you shouldn't roughhouse with her 'cause it would be, like, the more she got, the more she would have to have. But I don't believe that, because, when we started roughhousing with her, when she was a little thing and we found out she enjoyed this, I said to my husband, "We're touching her by doing this, we're socializing by doing this, we're teaching her language."

We do have respite. [It] works out good, because I pick my own people. I don't really use the people from the agency, even though I'm sure they're trained well. I'm sure the agency has checked into their backgrounds and everything. It's just, I feel a little nervous if I don't know the person very, very well. I use my sister-in-law, I use my best friend, and I use Jenny's aide who worked out so well for her last year. The aide left because, financially, she just couldn't make it on the pittance that they paid her. Jenny formed this really good bond with her, and she's really good with Jenny.

She sleeps at my mother's. Maybe every other weekend, she'll take a night and sleep over there. My mother has a little bedroom, a little spare bedroom for whoever is sleeping over, Jenny or Caroline. There's a little twin bed and there's toys, and my mother will sleep with her sometimes, or she'll sleep on the couch so she can hear her in there. She'll get her up in the middle of the night to go to the bathroom, the things that I would do.

Physically, she's very, very healthy, [but] she does have a condition in one of her eyes. One eye turns up and into her head, and she probably sees double vision, because she always closes her bad eye and uses her good eye, so she has a little Popeye face when she squints. You have to tell her to open her eye.

Stresses on the Family

My marriage has held up very well. For that I can be very thankful, because I know the odds were against us, as a couple, not as a family, but as a couple, because the stress of it all can do a number on your marriage. Instead of taking care of each other, you have this person that you have to be thinking about constantly, whether you want to or not. She's on my mind, and I can see where there would be some jealousy and some hard feelings and feeling left out and forgetting quality time and whatnot, but our marriage has held up remarkably well. I think we're stronger. I think we respect each other more. The love has always been there, but I think now there's more respect. There's just a bond between us.

I still got pregnant a second time, even though I knew something was up with Jenny, and that was nine months of agony. I worried big time. I can't do two of these kids, you know. I worried a lot, but I wanted two children. I was very paranoid [about Caroline, my second child]. And she had some speech problems that needed to be worked out. She went to speech therapy herself when she was two. A lot of things that hindered her development, speechwise, I think, were because of having an autistic sibling. Not that I want to blame Jenny for anything, but she did add to the problem. Caroline had trouble answering questions, 'cause she would repeat the question. I would say, "Do you want something to drink?" She'd say, "Something to drink." I'd say, "What do you want now?" She'd say, "Want now." I think part of it was developmental on her part, too, but part of it was that's how her big sister did it, so [that's how] she did it .

From what I understand, this is not necessarily a hereditary thing, and it's never been in our family that I know of, so Jenny's the first to be autistic. But they always ask you if there's any mental illness, on all those questionnaires that you have to fill out for school and whatever. There's always strange questions on there, like: Does anybody in your family have a mental condition? Why, what's that got to do with it? It's not schizophrenia here. I thought everybody knew that. You know, it's not in that category anymore. It's a physical problem of the brain, it's not a mental disease.

Long Range Forecast

[The hardest part about raising Jenny so far is] the emotional stress of worrying about her future, because there's no answers. There's many, many questions, but there's no real concrete answers. It worries me, 'cause I don't know how mainstreamed she'll be or could be. If she'll be able to be in a group home, or if she's going to be with me all the time, or if she's going to backslide and forget all these things that she knows right now. I don't know. I have no idea what to expect.

I mean, with Caroline, you don't always know what to expect with children, but you can pretty much gauge what might happen. I mean, she's going to kindergarten in the fall, and I know she's going on to first grade after that, and eventually she'll go to high school. I pretty much expect she'll have some grandbabies for me some day. I can't wait for that; it's something I can look forward to.

With Jenny, there's no knowing. Hopefully, she'll be integrated. Hopefully, she'll do well. Hopefully, she'll go on in school. These are all hopefullies. But then, after that, I don't know what to expect at all. I can't even hope.

Social Stigma

[In public,] it's her voice that is embarrassing, her little sounds. She'll go, "wooo wooo wooo," and gradually she'll get louder and louder. She stimulates herself with her sounds. It's always like a song, and it's always the same. She'll repeat a nonsense sound over and over again. Or she'll cup her two hands together over her mouth and yell to her ear, and that creates a really good echo. You'd think it would bust her eardrum, because it's so loud.

People start to look and stare, and I tell her, "Shh, you've got to tune it down, you've got to be quiet." Sometimes she just can't. Then she'll start laughing, and she'll get all goofy, and it's like, okay, how do I calm her down? Sometimes she'll get into a giggle fit, and I can't stop it. I've got to get angry. I've got to get firm with her and say, "You have to stop," and sometimes she can, and sometimes she can't.

[In a restaurant] other people in a kitchen cooking the meal can hear it. [But] we've never left. We've found a way to calm her down. When she was a baby, we'd give her napkins and she'd sit there and rip them open into little pieces. Everybody's napkins would get torn up into a little pile, and then I'd give her my keys, a tactic I still use. Something that worked when she was 18 months old still works now, when she's seven. I give her my keys, and she likes them. She likes my wallet, too, 'cause it smells like leather.

I try to redirect her, 'cause I don't want to pick her up and leave, because I know [that], being autistic, she may not want to do these things, but she can't help herself. Inside she must think to herself, I really shouldn't be doing this, but I don't think she always can control it. So it's not like she's always purposely trying to get into trouble or trying to embarrass her family or just act inappropriately. I just think she can't help it. So to get up and leave would be making her feel just that much more like she's different, [like] we can't handle her; we had to leave because of her, and I don't want to put that added pressure on her, so we usually stick it out. [It] makes me feel a little nervous, like I should be more in control, even though I know that this is the way she is and she can't help it. I shouldn't have all these guilt feelings that sometimes I do. It's hard to be always in control and never needing help. But she's never really gotten to the point where we've really gotten angry because she was really going off in a restaurant.

Basically, the neighbors know there is a problem but they're totally accepting of it. I really haven't had too much of a problem. The only problem I've ever had was when I had their pictures taken, several Christmases ago, at K-Mart. They were getting posed and the photographer was fixing her dress, and I told the photographer, I said, "You know, my daughter has autism, and she may not understand exactly what you're saying, but she will get your tone of voice, just speak in a proper tone of voice." I thought that was self-explanatory, you know, and after I said that, [the photographer] pulled back like she was going to catch something.

And this was back during the time when I used to cry about everything, so I went home and I cried, and I said, I can't believe this [woman] did this, I can't believe she did this. You know, if my daughter had something contagious, would I be bringing her to K-Mart, to have her picture taken? Would I be explaining it to her? And then I said, the hell with this, I'm not going to cry over this any more, I'm pissed. I was so mad, I went from crying on one end of the spectrum to the other end of the spectrum where I wanted to go back there and hurt this woman. Instead, I called up their main number for the photography place. I said, listen, we waited in line for three hours, first of all, with only three families in front of us. I said, when I finally go up there with my children, Jenny was very upset. She was getting very antsy, she was not very compliant and, I said, this photographer lady pulled away from [my] child like she was going to catch something.

Now, if that happened today, I would make fun of it, it would be nothing. It doesn't hurt my feelings anymore; it's just one more ignorant person that needs to be educated. But back then, it hurt my feelings so much I thought I was just going to die.

And then I said, no, I'm not going to feel this way. I'm going to get satisfaction. The pictures that came back were horrible, they were absolutely horrible, so I said, I'm calling these people back. So I did, and I wound up getting a free package deal. So the next time they had the photographer there, I went back. It was a different person, thank God [for the first photographer]. I would have said something to her. And the pictures came out a lot better. It was a gentleman this time, and he was very nice. He was very warm with Jenny, and he talked to her.

That's how I pick my doctor and everything else that involves Jenny—if the person is going to talk to her, instead of talking at her, then they're okay. If I have a dentist that's going to talk to me or talk at Jenny like she's not even there, then I'll find myself another doctor. But if they talk to her like she's a human being with feelings, who probably understands what they're saying, then that's probably a good doctor.

Surviving and Transcending

Jenny has taught us a lot. I used to be a little introverted, quiet, closed-mouth girl. I can't imagine myself being that anymore. You know, I used to be so quiet and shy and just content with being that way. But now I'm a little bit on the bitchy side. I know if I'm not that way, at least to a certain degree, I'm not going to get anywhere.

She's brought me out of myself, just like I'm helping to do for her. She's done that for me, and now I'm trying to do that back for her. She's made me very strong, she's made me very aggressive, something I never thought I would have to be. I never really cared, I had no reason to be. Now I have priorities.

And the one thing I've learned is that I really know the meaning of unconditional love. I know what that means now. I know full well what that means. You hear that, and you think that, oh yeah, I love you unconditionally, but I know exactly what that means now.

It means more than what you can imagine. Unless you have a little person who's very demanding, and live through some very, very, very hard times, you know, you go to hell and back, and you still love that person. How come? That's amazing, that I can say, not only do I love her, but, after what she put me through as a toddler, you know, the years have gone by since then, but I still like her, too. She's all right. You know, we get along really well. She's a goof-ball, and she's so much fun to be around. I mean, we fight and we have our problems, but she just makes me smile. I like watching her, because she's so different, it's intriguing and it's interesting.

I have to look at the good, because there's enough bad there to kill you if you dwell on it, so I look at the good. I used to do a lot of reading, but it was too depressing, because I read some of the wrong stuff. I read some of the old stuff. It was frightening: refrig-erator mother sort of thing. I read all I could get my hands on, and now I don't need to read anymore. Jenny's school has parents' meetings every month, and we get together and we talk, and I talk to my friends. Even though they really don't understand exactly what I'm saying, they're there to listen, especially my best friend.

She was here one day, and I had to take a shower, and she said she'd watch my kids, and I said, "No, you just watch Caroline. You have your baby to watch; I'll bring Jenny in the shower with me and I'll lock us in." Because I have a latch on the outside, so she can't get in [if I want to keep her out], and a latch on the inside, so I can lock her in if I want to. So I locked us in, and I'm taking a shower, and that day she was in a really horrible mood, and she screamed the whole time she was in there. And I just showered away. I've gotten so used to crying kids, it doesn't really bother me, where at one time it did. So I did my business, I shaved my legs, I washed my hair, I did everything I had to do and I got out, and I'm getting dressed and she's still screaming, and I opened the door and came out, and my girlfriend's sitting on the couch, and she's like, "I don't know how you do that, I don't know how you do that." I'm like, "Do what? What did I do? What did I do?" I thought maybe I forgot to put on a piece of clothing or something. What did I do? She goes, "How can you take a shower while she's in there screaming, without going insane?" I said, "My insane days were over a long time ago. I've learned to get over it. I've learned to push the off button, and I don't hear it anymore, when I have to." I needed a shower. I brought her in and just tuned out her screaming. So, when I got out and opened up the door, she had cried herself out, and she was okay. She just needed to get it out. When she cries like that, I just walk away and say, okay, cry, there's nothing I can do, so go ahead and cry. I've resigned myself to the fact she is going to cry and there's nothing I can do, so if I get all nervous, she's going to cry longer, and I'm going to have high blood pressure. So I let her cry and I walk away, and I just get mad at her when she throws things or if she bangs her head or something. I let her cry, as long as she isn't abusive. And then she usually stops on her own, and she's back to being all smiles and happy. So she just needs to get that out of her system.

[The advice I would give to parents who just found out their child had autism] would be, don't feel guilty for the feelings you have. There's going to be days when you might say, I hate this kid. I hate this kid. I want her gone. And don't feel guilty for that, because there are days when I've said, I can't stand this kid anymore. I went through so much, I mean crying constantly, I was a nervous wreck. I blamed everybody. I felt like I had done something wrong, so it's good, I think, to feel all those nasty feelings, 'cause if you bury them, don't feel them, when they do come out you're going to explode. So if you've got to cry, cry all you want. Just know inside there will come a time that you have to stop crying and you have to go on and find positive ways to deal with it. It's never all bad. You may feel that it's all bad, but there's some good there, so you've just got to look for it. I just look at her little face and I see these huge blue eyes and I say, God, she's beautiful. I make beautiful babies. You know, I do. I can't do a whole lot in this world, but I make beautiful babies. And I see all those little freckles that she got from my husband and the little dimples on her lower back that she got from my husband, and she walks the same way that he does, you know, she has the same stride when she walks, and she's made just like him, so on those really miserable days, I just look at her and say, yup, I want to kill her, but God, isn't she pretty. You just find the good, 'cause there's always good.

It's just sometimes the bad will seem to overshadow the good. You have to look even harder to see the positive, but it's there.

And they usually give you a lot back, a lot more than you think. You look where you've been, and you look where you are now, you usually find that you're a better person. You're stronger, you're more intelligent, you can handle crisis situations better, and you know how to love so much more. I love everybody in sight now. I have these motherly feelings I just can't bear. My girl-friend's pregnant, and I mother her to death. She tells me, stop, you've got to stop. Because of Jenny, people that I care about, I seem to mother, especially people that are there for me. And there was a time when I could not go to a person and say, "I love you," except my husband. And now I can go to my friends and say, "I love you." And there was a time when I couldn't say that, it was embarrassing or too hard for me to do. And because I love Jenny so much, I can love other people too. She broadened my heart, my mind, my soul, everything. She's all right. She's okay.

Chapter 3

The Wrestler

Bryant is a 9-year-old boy who lives with his father and mother, his 7-year-old brother, and his 2-year-old sister. The interview was with his mother in their home. Bryant's mother has returned to college to complete her degree in communications, and his father is in construction. Bryant arrived home about halfway through the interview.

Diagnosis

I first suspected something could be wrong during pregnancy, because I had toxemia very badly, and he stopped moving completely. I was on vacation in March, and he was due in two months. I ended up in the hospital down there, and they told me I had toxemia and to go home, but I came home and they did nothing. But Bryant didn't move from that day on. I went through all these tests, and they said, "He's fine, he's fine," but he was nonreactive.

He was born early, April 28th (because he was due May 19th), and they told me he was fine. But I don't know, when you go through a pregnancy like that, even though it was my first pregnancy, you worry a lot, even though they tell you he looks physically fine. I forget the date when babies are first supposed to make eye contact and all that stuff, but that's the first thing he didn't do. He didn't focus, he didn't follow. So my pediatrician sent me to an eye doctor, because they thought, possibly, he was blind. Well, all they determined from that was that they couldn't assess a 6-week-old, so that kind of left me up in the air. He had a hernia and hydrocele, so he had to have surgery right away. But then he went [along] pretty smoothly, so I thought, maybe it is just all in my head.

He did some things, he drank out of a cup very early, but he never stood up in his crib, and that's the first thing we noticed. You know, you get to these stages, and you expect that. We expected to go in one morning and have Bryant standing in his crib, and he never did it. Every morning we'd go in there, and he'd lay there. He sat up around the right time, but he couldn't eat. He wasn't swallowing his food right. He was on baby food until he was 2 ½ years old. So it was about that time that I went to my pediatrician, and he told me it was all in my head, I'm being a hyper-mother. And I really wasn't, I was the most relaxed mother. My sister was always kidding me [about it]. I just wasn't like that. He was a good baby, he never cried. There was nothing to be hyper about. He was a very content baby. You could do anything with him. The only thing that bothered him was touch, especially his face. You could not touch his face—he'd go spastic.

So I went for a couple more months, and then I went to a different pediatrician. It was like an emotional roller coaster. One day I'd wake up and say, he's fine, this was all in my head, and then the next day I'd wake up and say, I know there's something wrong with this child. My husband was great; he'd bring home all these books to show me that there was nothing wrong with him. He'd bring me home volumes, [but] it just wasn't a very big comfort, because for everything he'd bring me that would say he was fine, I could find just as many things [that said he wasn't].

Labelling

His first primary diagnosis was developmentally delayed. The autism [label] came much later. I finally got to a neurologist after the third time to the pediatrician. Bryant was 14 months old, and [the neurologists] knew the minute they saw him that something was wrong, before they even did a CAT scan. [The] CAT scan [showed] he has a large amount of brain damage on his left side, the Wernicke's area, so they told me that he would probably never speak. Even at that age, he was flapping [his arms]. They put in autistic-like behavior [on his diagnosis]. It was only three or four years ago that they actually gave him the label of autism.

Cause

They don't know [why I got toxemia]. I took really good care of myself. It was just one of those things. With Kevin, I had diabetes, but it wasn't too bad. With Kara, I had diabetes and toxemia, and I was in the hospital more than I was out, so no more kids. Kevin's hyperactive and on Ritalin. I'm not sure what causes that. I always think of him as healthy.

Grief and Sorrow

The neurologist—how this guy is still in practice is beyond me—called me on the phone to tell me he found this. I was pregnant with Kevin at the time, and he knew it, and he was so cold, and it was dreadful.

And I'm thinking, after I hung up, what am I going to say to [my husband] when he walks in the door? I didn't know how to say it except just to say it. He just went upstairs, and for two days I didn't see him. He just cried and he cried, and he just got out all his grief, and I said, that was the best, because I've been in groups, and I see the majority, and I mean the majority, of husbands are in denial. They refuse to accept what is going on, and they don't want any part of it, and there are more divorces over this, and I think we really hung together because of the way [my husband] handled it. And he got over his grief right away, and I thought that was tremendous.

I went, you know, through all the stages. I didn't really go through denial, but I went through grief and the mourning. I got him into an early intervention right away. The day after I left the neurologist, I was on the phone trying to get an early intervention program going. I'm a good one; when something's wrong, I can't get enough books and information on it. So I became very well acquainted with as much as has been written, which isn't all that much. This was brand new territory to me. This was really scary. The closest I ever had was a cousin with cerebral palsy, but we weren't close, so I saw him, maybe, once a year.

Day-to-Day Living

Bryant will be in bed by 7 o'clock. He isn't toilet trained for night, so his bed has to be stripped every morning, and he's still in diapers. He goes to bed pretty easily. He has a color TV in his room, and he has certain programs that he watches just about every night. And if they're not on—God forbid, if there's a special—all hell will break loose. Monday is MacGyver, and Tuesday is Rescue 911, and Wednesday is Flash—things that are fast moving, he likes, or things that have odd characters, he likes—he hooks right into it.

[If something is not on the night he expects it,] he'll usually start screaming. In fact, we just had to put him on medication. He can become very violent, throwing things, and usually directed at me. And he's big, he's up to here on me [*she puts her hand on her chest*], standing up. He's nine years old, and it was getting to the point where I couldn't handle it anymore, so I put him on Haldol. It's taken the edge off; it's calmed him down.

He can't dress himself or undress himself. He usually gets up around 7, and he just goes into the living room. He can't do anything himself, because he doesn't have the motor ability. So he'll just flap [his arms] and he usually flaps very quietly.

Eventually, while he's flapping, he goes through dialogues. He has a very good memory; they tell me it borders on genius. He takes paragraphs out of tapes. He has a whole library of tapes. I can usually pick up what tape or TV show he's dialoguing back and forth. His arms are up and he waves them. It's funny. When he was a baby, he used to close his fists and do this [*she waves*]. He could do that for two or three hours. I think that it's important for him to have what I call his flapping time, at least for him. So if he does it for half an hour a day, I don't mind it.

[Then I divert him.] He's diverted very easily, now that he's older. There were times when he used to spend practically his whole day flapping, but now that he's older [I can divert his attention to something else]. Thank goodness.

We have breakfast first. He's very reactive to foods. I could list on one hand what he eats. He vacillates with eggs. He goes through [a period] without touching them, then the next 6 months he will. And he drinks apple juice, milk, and water. That's it. He eats toast for breakfast and tuna and chips and three chocolate chip cookies for lunch, no more and no less.

Just the other day, I sent him a thermos of water, but when he came home, he told me about it. He did not like opening that thermos, and it had water in it and not apple juice. For dinner, he'll eat meats, no potatoes, no rice, no breads, just meat on a bone. We're battling right now for him to use a fork. [He just chews it off] like an animal. It's really disgusting. He'll eat steak, pork chops, [anything that has a bone in it]. My sister bought a special fork for handicapped people, the handle is very thick. It makes it easier to grasp, but he still doesn't want it. It always a battle. I think he can do it, he just doesn't do it. I think that it's amazing that he's as healthy as he is. And he's getting healthier and healthier.

I can give him chips in a bowl, and he'll have it all over everywhere and in his hair. I guess I'm just so busy, so I don't sit and watch what he's doing, and I can't understand how he can do that. [They're working on this at school.] Now he can sit here and eat spaghetti and not get it all over him, which is nice, because about seven months ago, I was coming to the point of forbidding spaghetti in this house, because it would be all over my floor.

That's another thing, five months ago, to go from one problem to another, he started vomiting. At first, I thought it was a virus. He lost seven pounds because he stopped eating. And then I noticed that he would vomit when he didn't like something. And when he didn't want to do homework, he'd force himself to vomit. We're still theorizing, still chasing down doctors, because he's still doing it. We're doing allergy testing. November to April, he's got a runny nose. Because of his problems, it's hard for him to blow his nose and get it all out, so a lot of it goes into his stomach. That was making him nauseous. And I think, in the beginning, he really was vomiting because he was physically ill. Now it's more like a learned behavior, 'cause he'll sit down sometimes and look at dinner, and this look comes across his face, and I know what is going to happen. And I'll say, "Bryant, go to the bathroom." You can't figure it out. The kid used to inhale milkshakes, and now he won't even look at one.

It was [happening every day], but [then] we started a new nasal spray from the allergist. I don't know if it's because his runny nose is gone, or that school's over and he doesn't have any homework, or that the medication is working or [that] it acts as a placebo. I took advantage of that, too. I told him the medication was going to stop him from vomiting. He believes everything you tell him. That's the nice thing about Bryant: I can tell him anything, and he takes it as gospel.

[After his breakfast,] we get into the shower. He enjoys his shower very much. It gives him another time where he goes through his dialogues. I go in with him and sometimes it's a nice time for us. Funny, for a baby that didn't like to be touched, he's a very huggy person. It's a time for us to spend time together, and sometimes we play games. He likes to play. He's very into wrestling, and sometimes he'll play that we're wrestlers coming into the ring.

He doesn't like [brushing his teeth]. Obviously, he doesn't care for anything in his mouth, and I have to do that. At school, he has to do it. But I do it here; someone has to do it, because trust me, taking him to the dentist is a lot worse. Three people have to hold him down at the dentist, because he just gets himself so worked up that he's gagging and he's crying. Thank God, a whole year and we've had no cavities.

The only thing he doesn't like [to wear] is his diapers at night. He's toilet trained during the day. It took him a long time, but he is. I think it was at four or five, more towards five.

[He really doesn't occupy himself.] I shouldn't say he'll do nothing—he will request a tape, but he could watch the same tape for 12 straight hours and keep rewinding that, but I just can't do that. Nothing interests him, no toys. Forget it, it's a waste.

[His brother,] Kevin, will initiate a game, and Bryant has to be just in the right mood. They like to play that they're pirates on a ship and the living room couch is one of the ships. Again, you have to catch him in the right mood and the right game. He'll never initiate it. Kevin tries to initiate, but if Bryant says no, Kevin knows that means no. He'll get him in a deadlock.

We went through a very bad time when Kara was smaller—thank God kids grow—where he would lead her into dangerous situations. Whether it was an adrenaline rush or what, he would lead her to staircases when she was a tiny baby, and still he takes her out to the road, if I leave them outside. We have a huge play center back there, just for the kids. But if she goes out with Bryant, you know that, within 5 seconds, she is going to be in the middle of the road.

And he knows it, 'cause he'll come back into the house and say to me, "Kara's in the road," 'cause he wants to see the whole action, what I'm going to do. So when she was a baby, I spent most of my days crying. We would just go from one episode to another that he would be doing with her: taking knives out of drawers and handing them to her. But she's cautious with him. She knows that he's hurt her and is not stopping, whereas Kevin knows where to stop. For being so little, she's really keyed into that. I've been lucky. Especially the times I found him opening the cellar door and taking her to the top of the stairs. Even now, he loves to tell her to take her clothes off, and he knows she's not supposed to do that. I'll tell you, for awhile there, I thought I was going to lose my mind. It was just so out of hand; it was an all-day thing.

Every year, as she gets a little older, it gets a little easier. I remember, when she just got home from the hospital, I walked in one day, and he had a pillow over her face. He was not real pleased when she came in the house. I was a nervous wreck with him and her together. It was a hard time, a very hard time.

At a very early age, God forbid that day, my husband turned on [wrestling]. He went click, by accident, because we don't watch it, and Bryant just [locked into it], and six years I've been locked into this crap. He gets the wrestling magazine, and he likes to look at the pictures.

We've been to one match. He enjoyed it. I've offered to take him to other matches; but unless Hulk Hogan is there, he doesn't want to go. He likes to go to movies; he likes to do family kinds of things. He's very oriented toward family traditions, like holidays and birthdays. [He likes] being with the family, doing things with the family, going camping. He loves to go camping. I'm trying to get one of those carriages you put on the back of your bike for him. He doesn't ride himself.

When he was younger, and I was attempting to teach him to ride the two-wheel bike and the training wheels, my mother came up here and tried to help and said, "Don't you worry, you're not going to fall, you're not going to hurt yourself." Ever since that day, and that was two years ago, that's all he talks about: "I'm going to tip over, I'm going to fall off." And he will not let go of that. You know, I'm not going to give up. I think one day I am going to get him to ride that bike. But, until then, I need something.

He likes to be in motion. At an early age, he went on the whip, and I had a stroke. They took him, at school, on the roller coaster—this is the big roller coaster. This is when he was in preschool, when he was 4 or 5 years old. I said, "God, Sharon, are you crazy?" She said, "He wanted to go on again." I said, "Good thing I wasn't there. I would have had a fit." I guess, when he was younger, he had no vestibular reaction. It seems his system is coming in now, and they can tell.

He just started [liking getting presents], and it's such a joy. Christmases were always hard, because I'm one of those people who puts months and months into Christmas. He knows what he's going to get. And you wrap it up, and he knows, pretty much, this is it. And it's hard to know what to do, 'cause if I give him the tape first, then he doesn't care about the rest of his presents. If I give him the tape last, all he's doing is tearing into the other presents to get to the tape. [That's the main thing he wants.]

People say to me, "What does he want for his birthday?" The tape is the cake, and what you get is the icing, and that might be insulting, but that's the bottom line. I don't know what to tell you. It's impossible to buy for Bryant, 'cause that's all he wants; he would be just as happy if he only got the tape. It takes very little to please him; the smallest things will please him. My family's pretty good; they got him Ultimate Warrior pajamas and a Hulk Hogan towel.

Halloween is a big deal for him. They have the party at school. Putting the costumes together takes about three or four weeks. It's hard to make a costume; especially because this year he wants to be The Flash. Do you know how hard that's going to be to do? But, once he gets his mind set on something like that, it's going to be very hard to change it, to talk him out of it. So actually, I should start thinking about it now, because I'm in school.

He likes the 4th of July, because he likes fireworks. When he was a baby, he hated them, he hated them: loud noises. Even now—you know I was just reading an article, [about] some work they're doing over in France, where they believe [that] if you can tone the eardrum to certain tones, it helps them deal with the autism. I don't know how much there is to this. But after [reading] the article, I've noticed that, still, if a plane's too low, he will cover his ears.

[He has an excellent memory.] He can tell you things that someone said to him on his third birthday. It's the most amazing thing. You know, sometimes I can really stretch my memory and think, son of a gun, that really did happen. So now I just take what he says for gospel. Because you're going to find, the majority of times, he's right.

[At school,] he walks into a classroom. He's mainstreamed now, second year of being mainstreamed. By the second day, he can tell you everybody's name in there. He's very good with names, and maps. Highways are a particular love of his: where they run; exits. The [ones on the Massachusetts Turnpike] are his favorites. He knows the titles, but I'm not sure he understands [what they mean]. He still has a lot of trouble recognizing letters and numbers. They all seem to be Greek. He can read things on a map, but, in another context, he might not know them at all. Things like McDonald's, he can spot that two miles away. He is fantastic at logos: the colors and the way they're written. And they think that's how he's going to learn how to read, in one batch. Any other way is just not working.

We just went on vacation to the Cape for a week. For the first time in my life, I realized how really empty Bryant's world is, how little he enjoys. We're going to all these places, and I thought there would be something there that interested him, but he could have cared less. It was sad for me. It was a hard day. I say, all the time, thank God for Kevin. I could share all this with Kevin. We're going to Pennsylvania in August, and I'm kind of glad we went to the Cape: at least I'm not setting myself up for disaster, at least I know what to expect. Bryant's not going to care about the Liberty Bell.

He'll start singing with me in the car, 'cause he knows all the words. I love to play the game with him, Whose Singing This Song? [Also,] he'll tell you the titles. We went to the fireworks the other night, and it'll come to me, not the Battle Hymn of the Republic, [but] another national-type song, and his father said to him, "Do you know that song Bryant?", and he spit the title right out. You know, he picks up so much information, you don't even know. I'm surprised that he knew that song, because it's not one that you hear an awful lot.

This is the first year in his life he actually picked up a pencil and drew from one dot to another, and we're all ecstatic. This is big time, because we never thought he'd be able to do it. He's so tactile defensive. You know, he just doesn't want anything in his hands. Even when he was in preschool, the tables and the water tables—he doesn't like to play in water. Even washing his hands, he's not real thrilled with.

[Another thing is money.] Money has absolutely no meaning to him: you could give him $100, $5. You give him the smallest thing, and he's happy. Of course, there's Kevin, so there's an advantage to [this but] a $10 bill would be the same as an 80¢ package of M&Ms. [When he was attending] a lower level in school, they tried using the token system. He could never even understand that. He wants immediate gratification. One of the foods that he adores is M&Ms.

[One thing he can do is talk.] The doctors told me he would never speak. [But he started when] he was 2 years and 2 months. He's 9, but his speech is on a 6-or-7-year level. His speech is good, you can understand him. But for content, it's very interesting. On the surface, if you listen to Bryant, it's amazing how well he talks. If you listen to his content, most of it is things that he's heard. And sometimes it'll just hit me: the sentence he just gave me, I said three days ago. He takes these and plunks them in the right places, but his speech is not Bryant-generated speech. As a matter of fact, I was just saying that to my therapist. The more I watch this child, it is fascinating how empty his speech actually is, [but] he gives the appearance of speaking so fluently.

Lot of times, I'll say, "Bryant, what did you just say?", and he'll say, "I'm just talking to myself." That's a new thing. I've never heard him say that before to me. But then again, I'm not sure if that's Bryant-generated or that's Mom-generated.

He has a lot of [repetition]. He perseverates now on paragraphs, thank God. He used to perseverate on words, until you thought you were going to take him and strangle him or stuff something in his mouth. A phrase like, "I want to go now, I want to go now," and he would just go on and on and on and on and on, until you just thought you were going to burst. At least now it's whole paragraphs. That I can tolerate, that doesn't even bother me.

[Another thing he does is] ask the same question [over and over again]. I find that very difficult. After the tenth time of being asked the same question, I start to lose it a little. "What time is Daddy coming home?" Ten minutes later: "What time is Daddy coming home?" Five minutes later: "What time is Daddy coming home?" It's almost like a game, because he knows the answer, because a lot of times, instead of [telling him, I ask him:] "What did I tell you?", and he can answer me. The other night we had company for dinner. God forbid, they were two hours late. "What time are they coming?" Two hours I listened to this. "What time are they coming?" And he wouldn't accept the fact that they had called and said they would be late. He just didn't care.

He says these outrageous things, but I don't think he really understands [them], like, "I'm going to kill you with a knife. I'm going to cut your head off." He loves to swear, because he loves the reaction, although it has cut down dramatically. I guess he saw that I really meant business about this subject. He called me a bitch.

His inflection is pretty flat, and his facial expression is just about the same. I went to sign language classes, but we never had to use it. He hated signing anyway, so [I didn't push it]. I think his voice is louder than normal. He has no conception of what I mean when people are sleeping and I say, "Lower your voice." I'm not sure he knows how to do it. I'm not sure I know what the problem is. He can't whisper. Physically, maybe, he doesn't know how. I don't know.

I'm just teaching him how to talk on the phone. It's still a very hard concept for him. I mean, Bryant knows everybody, and everybody knows Bryant. I have to say, "Bryant, say hello." He'll mumble it.

If he wants to say something to you, he'll say something to you. He can easily come in here and totally ignore you and go into the living room. That's something they're working on in school:

what you're supposed to say when you leave a room, but the process is slow.

He really takes in the world [using mostly his] auditory [faculties]. They tell me he's more in the minority for that, [that] usually kids are visual learners. To be an auditory learner is not that popular. So most of the programs that are out there are visual, visual, visual, like the computer.

[He also seems less sensitive to some things.] When we first moved in, we were poor. Well, we're still poor [*she laughs*]. And we had a kerosene heater. And my sister had it, and it worked really well. Except, one day, Bryant walked in and put his hand on the heater and walked over to his father and said, "Look Daddy, I burned my hand." He burned it and he never cried—third degree burns. He never cried. He can do things to himself that I could never stand. But, on the other hand, he'll imagine all these [bad things]. I tell him [that], if I'd let him, he'd turn into a hypochondriac. "My knee hurts, my toe hurts." Everyday, we hear this at least three or four times a day: my head hurts, my eyes are watering. All these imaginary things, but when it comes to reality, and something is really happening with his body, [there's no reaction].

He's had a lot of surgery. He didn't have a lot of pain. If he did, you didn't know it. His pain tolerance is incredible. I wish I could be like that, I really do. [But] for awhile I was really concerned about how was he going to know when he really got hurt. I suppose it's something he'll just learn. I don't know. It's really hard to know [if he's sick] unless he has a fever. A lot of times, he just won't even complain.

[But he will let you know how he feels about you.] He's the kind of kid that he either likes you or he hates you, and that's it. We've had a lot of problems with aides, because, if he decides he hates you, that's very difficult. He's decided that he really likes Tammy, and I say every day, "Thank God, he likes her."

[*His aide, Tammy, comes in with Bryant and says,*] Today was a little weird. I think he was really tired. We went to open swim. He went in, but he was grabbing my throat, and I said, "Don't do that, you'll hurt somebody." Then he would do it again, and it would hurt, so I pulled his hands, and he started hitting me, and then he got all mad. So we put him in time out. That's all you can do, just put him in time out. [*Bryant says,*] "I don't like you anymore."

[*Bryant's mother resumes speaking.*] He's affectionate, and if he likes you, it's going to be 100%, and it's difficult. [For example, he was very affectionate with] the company we had for dinner the other night, and it's hard on them, and it's hard on me. There are very few people that come here that don't [push him off]. It was okay until he was five. I think it says a lot about our society. Usually he'll get sad, he'll take it as rejection.

He depends on me. Mommy can always make it better. It's a very special relationship. In one way, it's nice. I'm glad that, at least, I can calm him down, but, on the other hand, it's scary that I'm the only person that can do it.

[Although he's affectionate with people,] he is absolutely terrified of [other] living creatures. Dogs—because they're common I say dogs, but it could be a cat, it could be a rabbit, it could be an ant. If it's living and moving, he starts crying and screaming, "Get me away from there," and he will physically get himself as far away as he can. And nothing bad has ever happened, so I'm not sure where the fear comes from. But he just won't have any part of it, and the more I try to desensitize him, the worse it gets.

[He also gets mad sometimes.] If he gets really mad, he'll bang himself on the head, but not so hard that he'll cause damage. He's got his sister doing it; it's funny. She gets really mad, and she'll say, "Oh fine," and she [will hit herself on the head].

I get kicked. He hits mostly and kicks. I usually have my share of bruises. He's gotten my sister and my mother in a choke hold, because he knows all the wrestling moves, and he's liable to hurt you. He used to bite terribly, but he hasn't done that since he was 3. But he does throw things, anything he can reach. And he gets extremely verbal when he's angry. "I'm going to kill you. I hate you." He tells you all the things he's going to do to you that he's heard from movies and tapes. "I'm going to cut your head off." His new one is: "I'm going to rape you," although he has no idea what it means. And I can't figure out where he heard that one. I said to him the other day, "You don't even know what it means." But that's his new one; for the last couple of days I've heard that one quite a bit.

He has never hurt anyone seriously, but I think he's got the potential and definitely the strength. He's much stronger than I am. That's why I went to the neurologist and said, you have to give us something. And Haldol's really taken the edge off. He's not as mad as he used to be. Bryant is getting big, and I'm getting concerned about [it]. In a couple of years, I'm not going to be able to do this any more. He's going to have me in a choke hold, and he's going to strangle me, and that's going to be the end of me. And I'm not joking, I'm being very serious.

Treatment

I'm not really a good believer of behavior modification [or] behavior modification specialists. It makes no sense to him. I have all my little charts and all my stars and my stickers. Do you think he really cares? You can behavior mod until next year, and, I'm sorry, I have just not seen it work. Schools are big believers in it, and they have this big integration specialist [who] is a big believer in it. My husband and I said, "We'll listen to you, but sorry, we really don't believe this stuff." The kid could be timed out for the next seven years. He doesn't care, he just doesn't care. He'll come out and start the same behavior he was timed out for. And working toward something? No way.

They used to always tell me [medications] wouldn't work. They weren't living with him. I figured that, by the time [behavior modification] started working, I'd be 100. I figured I had to take things into my own hands here [and get him on medication].

[*Bryant comes out with his pants half way up.*] I want you to go back and flush the toilet. [*Bryant says,*] "I love you." [*His mother says,*] "I love you too sweetheart, very much. Go flush the toilet."

There are sometimes, especially near the end of the day, where I'd do anything just to shut him up. It's awful, but I'm really tired. Bryant has patience that most humans would not understand. He can outwait you, trust me, any day of the week. So there are sometimes that I just can't outwait him anymore.

He's mainstreamed, [and] he'll be going to third [grade] next year. He has one aide with him throughout the whole day. He likes being with typical kids. He loves it. He's changed so much. I wish I had a before-and-after video. The hairpulling and the biting: all this disappeared when he got into a regular school and he saw that that was not appropriate behavior. He's modelling typical kids now.

[But] we had some troubles with the teacher this year. It's a long story; she didn't want Bryant in the classroom, so we had problems there. She took Bryant in the classroom because it was the only way she was going to get her job back. That was the ultimatum that was given to her. She had gone on a leave. That feeling [of trouble] went through the whole year, because she didn't want him, and she made everybody miserable, mostly me. She's young too. That showed me something about age, because the teacher that wants him for third [grade] next year is 60 years old, so that really taught me a lesson.

Stresses on the Family

It's a stress on a marriage, no doubt about it. My husband still talks about how Bryant's my favorite, between him and Bryant. [*She laughs*].

[It affects the siblings too.] Kevin, a couple of years ago, asked me, "Mom, when I turn 6, am I going to have brain damage?" When he was younger, [he asked me,] "Mom, when I turn 4, am I going to drool?" Those things, you know, they're thinking.

Kevin knows where Bryant's brain damage is and what happened to him, and he knows the whole nine yards, but sometimes he really gets confused. So I try to talk to him, of course, "You're not going to drool. That's part of Bryant's problem. He can't swallow like you and I do, so he drools. That's not going to happen to you." And I've had Kara coming up [and asking me questions], and I think I'm going to be going through the same thing, [although] it may be different, because she's female.

When he was younger, my family took him more. My sister used to take him for a week in the summer, and even up to last year, when she didn't have my father [to take care of (he has Alzheimer's)], she took him for a week. When I pick him up, I get to hear about all the awful things he did. I always feel like I'm really intruding and I shouldn't be doing it.

[For example,] my husband and I just went away for the weekend, and we were gone three days, and my niece took the kids. And although she was getting paid quite a bit of money for it, through respite, when I came home, she said, "Oh, I'm so glad you're home." And I got a litany of all hell [having broken loose], so I have mixed feeling about it. I'm not really comfortable. It's not easy for me to ask.

The babysitter last night is not competent to handle him anymore. You should have seen what I came home to. I don't need that, and my husband didn't have to come home to it [either]. I mean, the whole bathroom and my living room were torn apart.

I can see a bunch of kids his age playing baseball, and it can still make me cry. Or he can have awful [arm] flapping, and that can make me cry. Sometimes you think you're over that, but my girlfriend has this great line. She says, "We don't learn to ever accept this; we just learn to live with it." And I think that is so true.

Long Range Forecast

I'm hoping that he can hold a job. He's not going to live alone, I know that's a reality. I don't think he'll ever have the concept of money or be able to take care of his own needs totally, but I'm hoping he can live away from me.

Social Stigma

I don't think he sees himself as different, and I think that's been hard, because the neighborhood kids really don't want to play with him, and he doesn't understand why. He doesn't see himself in terms of being different than the rest of the world.

I watch a lot of people watching him, which is very fascinating, because you know that they know that something is wrong, but they don't say anything, and they're trying to figure out what's wrong.

Sometimes it would be better if he were outright just physically disabled, because people make all these exceptions. [*The interviewer says,* "When you have someone like Bryant they think he's just a normal kid being bad."] That's right. That's exactly right.

Surviving and Transcending

You know, sometimes [you think] living with [a kid with autism] is normal, and it takes something to wake you up and say, hey, this isn't normal. It's true: every 6 months I need to be hit in the head and say, listen, this isn't the way everybody else lives, you know.

[The advice I would give parents who just found out their child had autism] is get into a parents' support group. Talk to parents. It's a very lonely feeling. It's not like you can go to your neighbor and say, "Bryant just had a bowel movement all over my rug," which used to be an everyday event for me. He used to take his diaper off and go all over my rug every single day. It was such a frustrating time in my life. It's very lonely, unless you've got an exceptional family. They say, "Oh yeah, I understand." They don't understand. They're not living it. So I would say, get support because if you don't get support, I see marriages fall apart, I see people fall apart. I think the most important thing is: just get support.

Just seeing that someone else is living with it, and they are doing it, gives you a lift. It's true. It's true. Hanging in there. You can't get that from a book. Although books certainly do have their place.

You get new ideas. Like Bryant's surgery—having his [parotid] glands removed—I got that from a parents' support group. I don't know if I ever would have heard that. They found out there was no harm in removing them, because you have so many other glands, and he's not dry, and there's been absolutely no side effects.

It's not that you need a support group because you haven't accepted the problem. That's not the issue. The issue is [that] you're going through different stages, and [at] every stage you have new problems and new issues. You just get through one, and you say, "Ah," and then you come up to another, and then you say, "Oh God, now what do I do?" It's the support and the suggestions [that help you get through it].

You'd never go to a parents' support group and have some-body say, "It could be worse." That's one thing you just do not say. I can't believe it when people say that to me. Like, I could be dead. So what?

I think it's given me an [awareness of the] value of life I never would have had. I just know I wouldn't have. You truly don't appreciate what you have until you don't have it. [Having been through what I've been through with Bryant, I'm] just appreciating life to its fullest.

He's made me—not that I always wasn't—be more outgoing, more confident. I think I've done a really good job with him, considering [that] when they gave me his diagnosis, [they] told me I was dealing with a child that couldn't talk, couldn't eat, couldn't walk, you know. Everything I've worked for and gone through with him has given me a special [awareness of the] value of life and a closeness to him. I mean, I love my other children dearly, but it's just not the same as with Bryant. Well, he looks just like my father, which has a lot to do with it, but we have a very special relationship, just by virtue of Bryant being Bryant.

Chapter 4
The Groom

 Arthur is a 16-year-old boy who lives with his father Dan, who has primary custody of him. They live adjacent to Cassy, who is Dan's partner. Arthur has a 22-year-old brother, Roland, who is living on his own, and a mother, Julie, who sees him on alternate weekends and on vacations. The interview was with Dan, who is a vice principal at an inner-city high school. We met at his home while Arthur was at work.

Diagnosis

Although Arthur had a normal delivery and no physical problems at birth, he reacted really badly about having his diaper changed, from day one. It was like you were twisting his arm. He would scream about being on his back. Any normal kid would just like to lie down. He wouldn't. He wanted to be held up while his diaper was changed.

And he was very irritable all the time. He would get into a crying fit, and it would be really hard to get him out of it. Everyone was saying he was colicky, but he wasn't. It was a pattern that no one knew anything about. You'd go to the pediatrician, and they'd say, "Relax; buy him a swing or something." By 4 or 5 months, Julie was telling the pediatrician something was wrong. I was saying, we've got to give it time. I was the one who was saying, we've got to get through this, that there are all kinds of babies, and some are easy and some are tough, and it's not going to be like Roland. Everything else about him appeared to be perfectly fine: his weight, or the way he ate, everything else was fine.

The pediatrician said, you're overreacting, the same stuff I was saying, all babies are different, and you've got to get over this, there will be another phase. And [she] scolded us as parents for not biting the bullet. She was an old German woman, and she would say things to us like, "Shame on you. This isn't your first baby; you should know better than this."

I think she retired, so we went to [another pediatrician]. He didn't have any answers either, but you had the sense that he would listen. And I think he was the one who referred us to [the hospital for the evaluation]. Arthur was about 2, 2 ½ then. Actually, we went to a psychiatrist first, and he observed Arthur in play, and his basic theory was that he hadn't gone through certain developmental stages yet. He would say things like, give him a garbage can and let him throw it upside down and throw garbage all over the place, saying somehow he hadn't gone through that stage yet. The major emphasis was [that] somehow we had really screwed up with this kid, and he was going to help us have Arthur go through these stages that he hadn't been able to, under our tutelage.

Labelling

Either this psychiatrist or the hospital was the first to mention the diagnosis of autism. The only idea I had about autism at that time was some kid sitting in a corner banging his head and definitely avoiding touch, and that wasn't Arthur. When he was real young, he would cling to you, almost like he was dead. There was no body support of his own. He was, like, stuck to you; it was just like wearing a sack of flour. The anti-touch stuff was something that made no sense to me at all. The major thrust was, though, whether you want to call it autism or not, that he had, most likely, a lifelong disability that would affect his intelligence and everything else.

Cause

[We're not sure what caused Arthur to be autistic, but] during her fifth month of pregnancy with Arthur, Julie became ill with a high fever, nausea, and double vision. We were visiting some friends on the Cape. She was hospitalized for two weeks, but the condition was never diagnosed, and the conclusion at the time was that the fetus had not been harmed. And when Arthur was born, he appeared normal, and his Apgar scores were very good.

Grief and Sorrow

I think we were both pretty numb [when we first heard it]. Up until that point, I just denied a lot of stuff. I just said, well, it will get better. I would come home from [work], and Julie would be a mess, and she said, "You take care of him." She wanted to know what was wrong. But after this doctor at the [hospital] stated it, I never fought it anymore.

Right away, after we had Arthur, I really wanted to have another child. I think it is kind of this reaction [of] wanting to balance things out or something, but we never really did it. This just existed in my own mind; it was never really talked about. I don't know what Julie was thinking. I think it's almost like a natural thing: you want to straighten something out. Other than that thought, I would say that I was determined not to have any more.

When it crosses my mind [now, I think] it's worse now than it was as he was growing up. There was more hope [then]. People would say, we hope to be able to do this and this. When he was about two, you could practically state an entire paragraph and he could repeat it. He knew the alphabet song way before any kid, even before Roland knew the alphabet song, even before a lot of kids were talking. He used to have some real talents, whether it was just memorization or whatever. Some people were saying, this kid is obviously a genius. But then he stopped talking all together.

When he started to get into some of the educational stuff, his speaking was all garbled and backwards, but you could see some movement, so you thought, when he gets this together, he's all of a sudden going to take off. These are just little fantasies that you have. It was always the hope that once you got over this hurdle, maybe the wiring would somehow get together and he would really blossom. And it was just enough change and movement to keep that line going. [But] after he learned to read, there wasn't a lot of change, really. It's struck me more in the last two or three years, now that he's six feet tall and looks like an adult: So here's what his body is basically going to look like for the next 50-odd years. And that's harder to handle. As he's growing up, you see him and he's 12, getting taller, and the next year there's all this growing stuff. Then, when that starts to slow down, I think the expectations kind of start to slow down.

Day-to-Day Living

Just a few years ago, Arthur would be up all night talking to himself or singing loudly, and he seemed to hardly sleep at all. When he was younger, he had to be locked in his bedroom or he would get up in the middle of the night and wander, even outside. He is now able to sleep through the night, from 10 or 11 until morning. He still sleeps with a light on, and he still insists on wearing clothes to bed. Usually, what he does is shower at night and change his clothes. Then those clothes are the ones he wears to bed and the next day. He is very defensive about talking about this subject, and he will get visibly upset and angry if you bring it up. [He says,] "You do not talk about me!" He also locks himself in his room with two locks, although you could get in if you needed to.

He dresses himself, and he has definite preferences. He will only wear certain colors. White is his favorite, but he will also wear red, grey, or black. He will refuse to wear blue, but if you tell him that it's not blue, that it's turquoise or azure, then he will wear it. I buy all his clothes for him. He insists on wearing new clothes everyday and spends a lot of time washing clothes and talking about what goes into washing clothes, like different types of detergents. He likes to wear sweatshirts over his shirts and he'll be angry if you suggest he take it off on hot days, although he usually complies after a while. He'll button up his shirt all the way to the top, and he'll tuck his sweatshirt into his pants. You can tell him it looks odd, but he will argue with you that this is not true, or he will say, "No, it looks Audi."

As of the last couple of years, we have been trying to talk to him explicitly about his autism. One time, we composed a typed sheet for him, entitled, "Questions and Answers about Autism," and we left it out on a table where he could find it. He is less defensive when he reads something. When he was younger, you could talk about him right in front of him and it wouldn't have mattered, he wouldn't have been paying attention, but now he is more aware that he has a handicap and that he is not typical, although he will often argue with you about whether something is typical or atypical. If, for example, he is licking his soda bottle, and you tell him not to do that, that it is atypical, he will say, "No, it is not," and he may call you a liar. He sometimes says what we do is "a-handicapped."

He is starting to eat a greater variety of food, but spaghetti and meatballs is still his favorite. He will invariably end up with some of it on his clothes and on his face and will need to be prompted to clean his face with a napkin. Up until a few years ago, he would leave a mess on the table and all around the place where he was sitting. He likes to go out to restaurants, and he does order for himself, but he rushes to be the first one to order.

He is very interested in beverages. For one thing, he drinks lots of water all day long, and he insists on using a clean glass each time, so there's this trail of glasses on the counter and in his room. He also wants a jug of water by his bed at night and whenever he knows we are going on a trip. His favorite beverage is Dr. Pepper. He has even written to the company to get literature, and one of his dreams would be to visit a Dr. Pepper factory. He often gets Dr. Pepper six-packs for one of his Christmas presents, and he is very happy with them. For a while, he insisted on having diet Coke when we went to restaurants, and if they didn't have it when he ordered, he would start making such a fuss that we had to leave. To avoid this, we would have to talk to the waitress or waiter ahead of time, and tell them to call whatever cola they had, diet Coke. He could never taste the difference. We use that same ploy with other foods. It's often more the idea or the label of something, rather than the reality.

If he sees any new beverage brand, he has to try it, and he is very into knowing the names of nonalcoholic beers. He's also very obsessed with soda machines. If we travel anywhere, his major interest is in finding a soda machine, learning what types of beverages are in there, and how much they cost. This is usually much more important to him than the sights.

[To help Arthur occupy himself,] we bought him his own remote-controlled TV set for his bedroom, this last Christmas. It was one of our best purchases. It allows us to have some respite from him. He will now spend time by himself, in his room, while in the house. His favorite shows are: America's Funniest Home Videos, Erkel, and Life Goes On. Prior to that, he would have to be where you were and preferably talking at you, unless he was outside and engaging in some project he thought up, usually involving water (like watering plants or washing the car) or cutting down or transplanting weeds. He wants us to buy him a weed remover he's seen advertised on television, but we're afraid he would defoliate the yard if he got one.

Not that long ago, he would be distressed to receive presents. We would have to find out what he wanted, and then show it to him, and then wrap it up with him looking. It's only in the last few years that he likes surprises. Even now, he does not let us celebrate his birthday. We got a dog a few years ago and have a big party for him, which is really, in disguise, a party for Arthur.

On occasion, he will agree to go to the movies with us, but, more often than not, it's a Disney movie or a cartoon, although he did like Home Alone and the Ernest movies. He has a problem in video rental stores, because he wants to do what teenagers do and not what kids do, but the movies he prefers are usually found under a sign that says, Children's Section, so he can't pick them. Again, we usually have to trick him to get him what he wants.

He has also developed an interest in automotive vehicles in the last few years. He says he has figured out, from looking at vehicles and seeing if they are new or old, what models have been discontinued, and he can rattle off a list of 30 or so from memory.

He is also very concerned about the number, type, and location of the windshield wipers on each type of vehicle. He is especially interested in [expensive cars with] windshield wipers on headlights. When we were on vacation this summer, we gave him a Polaroid camera to play with, and he took a picture of a car in the parking lot, a Mercedes, with headlight wipers. The odd thing is, though, if you ask him why he is interested in wipers, he will say he is not, that he doesn't like them and that they get in the way of your seeing. Yet he is always talking about them.

One of his major upsets this year was the fact that he turned 16 and couldn't get a license. He had no real understanding that he wouldn't be able to do this, and he had just assumed he would get it like his brother had when he turned 16. He had even called a driving school and left a message, on their answering machine, to call back. He was very upset about this, mostly because he felt he would not be a grownup unless he had a license. Telling him about other adults who didn't have a license didn't help. He went through every emotion with this, from crying to becoming very belligerent. This summer, he got a fishing license, and that sort of helped a bit; at least he got a license.

He also talks about getting married someday and getting a marriage license. This is another one of his obsessions right now. Again, this has to do with becoming a grownup. He says he is getting married in white at a formal wedding at a park near our house. He has picked out what food will be served (spaghetti, of course) and who he is going to invite and not invite. At a restaurant recently, after he had ordered spaghetti, the waitress said to him, "And you would have to be wearing white." And he turned to me and asked for reassurance, "But I'm still going to be having spaghetti at my wedding?" He tells people he is going to get married, but he is not going to have any sex. He told this to Cassy's brother, and he added that it's not uncommon, that lots of people don't have sex: for example, Cassy doesn't. We thought this was pretty funny, and after asking him some more questions about who did and didn't have sex, we figured out what he meant. Sex meant having babies, and if you didn't have any children, you didn't have sex.

You have to understand that he talks about getting married many times a day and to whomever he can get to listen to him. He usually doesn't introduce what he is talking about; you just have to figure it out as you go along. He always tells the same story: he will be wearing white, having spaghetti, etc., and even if he has told you this same exact story 700 times before, and this is no exaggeration, he will tell it to you again with the same animation and tone as if it were the first time. Most people politely listen to him. If you challenge him by saying, "You already told me that before," he will become "very angry," as he puts it, and say, "Shut up, I don't care." If you tell him typical people usually only tell the same story once to other people, he will challenge you. Once recently, however, I asked him if he didn't remember telling me, and he said no, he was sorry, he didn't remember. It is hard to know if he really doesn't remember telling you or if he does, but enjoys repeating it. He also talks about events that happened many years ago, again, as if they just happened or as if you weren't there. Sometimes he enjoys changing the characters around, especially if he's telling the story of something he did wrong. "You said a bad word, Cassy, you did," or "You spilled the juice on the floor on purpose."

That's another thing he used to do, and still does, to a certain extent, now. If you accidentally spill something or drop and break something, he will repeat the action and say you did it on purpose and he did it by accident. He acts almost as if the restrictions on bad behavior are lifted, and he is most gleeful about it.

He will also perseverate on one phrase, but now he just repeats something 5-10 times. When he was younger, he just seemed like he could go on forever. Now you can usually stop him by telling him you heard him, although you will probably still get the "I don't care" response. I read in a few places that kids with fetal alcohol syndrome are also fond of the "I don't care" expression.

He engages in a lot of word play. [He will say,] "I took off the *F* (of the restaurant, Friendly's) and it became Rriendly's." He also likes to rhyme words. Many of these creations are nonsensical, but occasionally he creates new words that are amusing. He told his brother he was so annoyed with him, he was Illinois-ed. And recently, he said he doesn't believe in capital punishment, but he does believe in lower case punishment.

He has a couple of words that he refuses to say correctly, even though he can. He says *abular* for *regular* and *radish* for *rather*. When he was much younger, he referred to Abraham Lincoln as Regular Ham Linkland, and he says now that, since he used the word *regular* then, he can't use it now. He also says the words *regular* and *rather* by themselves bother him when he says them. It's hard to know, however, if these are the real reasons, because usually he refuses to answer any why questions, and any answer you get is usually after much prompting.

One of the most disturbing habits he has now is his verbal threats and swearing. Utterances that he has heard loudly or emphatically in the past, he will repeat with the same intonation, but totally out of context. Some of his favorites are: I'm going to cut off your head; I wish you were killed; I'm going to pick up some dog poop and put it in your mouth; and You're evil, I'm going to lock you in a closet and throw away the key. Although he has never acted on any of these threats, he says them in a very menacing way, almost as if he were possessed. Some of these expressions he has copied from his classmates, some he has heard on television. Oftentimes, he learns new expressions by saying one of these gems to a classmate, who then responds in kind. It is very hard to reason with him that these are inappropriate expressions, because he has heard them from people that are supposedly normal. Fortunately, if not tempted, he confines most of this language to us and does not say it in public.

Another thing he will do which can be annoying is he will laugh if you say you are hurt or in pain. He never has a natural laugh; it is a very contrived "ha ha ha," with a smile. If you tell him it is not appropriate to laugh at someone else's pain, he will say, "I don't care." If you say, "How would you like me to do it to you?", he will say, "You do not do this." If you do anything to him that he does to you, you will pay dearly. The lesson is lost. We have tried to teach him the golden rule, but he has made up his own rule that he calls the silver rule, which is: he is the only one who can do this, no one else is allowed.

He is also obsessed about washing his hands. He washes [them] many times a day, and when he does, he does it like a surgeon, meticulously and way above the wrists. He also uses very hot water, so his hands come out beet red. I don't think he can feel the difference.

Most of his aggression today is verbal. He will, on occasion, throw something at you, like a pencil, or slap or pinch you, but it usually does not hurt. When he was younger, before he became a teenager, he would have furious temper tantrums, where he'd be flailing at you and screaming and kicking and biting and pinching and throwing things. This could go on for an hour or more. These could be provoked by [seemingly innocuous events, such as] asking a question, like, "Do you want a Pepsi?", because he doesn't like Pepsi. He could yield tremendous power with these tantrums, so you didn't want to do anything to provoke one. I would have to take him to a quiet spot and try to calm him down. For a long time, Cassy was afraid to turn her back on him.

He can also be affectionate, and will hug anyone who asks for one, but, usually, he holds his body stiff while he hugs. Most of the time, his body tone is just the opposite, very loose. He has even been referred for scoliosis testing, because he stands so slouched, but the tests were negative. He sits in a very relaxed posture and can sit in one place, doing nothing, for long periods of time without showing any signs of boredom. As a matter of fact, it seems most times he would prefer to be doing this. When he does walk, his gait is off. He doesn't have a smooth stride. You can tell from looking at his posture and movements that something is wrong.

He has no sense of time, even though he can tell time. For example, he reads on his mouthwash bottle that you should wait 30 minutes before eating or drinking for maximum effectiveness. After two minutes has passed, he will ask us if 30 minutes have passed and it is okay to eat, and will believe us if we say yes.

He still has problems with safety, although it is better. He used to just run out into the street without looking to see if a car was coming or not. Now he overcompensates and keeps looking back and forth, back and forth, which looks very odd, but at least is more safe.

He has no one that calls him, other than his relatives, but there are a few people, previous school counselors and respite workers, he will call. Sometimes he calls just to announce something that has happened in the family; other times he will call for another opinion. He was doing this a lot when we first told him he couldn't get a license. He doesn't have any friends that he's made on his own and resists if we ask him to bring someone along. "Ah, ah, I'd radish not."

The hardest thing about Arthur is his resistance. It seems that he has learned almost nothing about the world on his own. Unless you've have been around a kid with autism, you don't realize how much you learn about the world just by watching others and asking questions, both of which Arthur doesn't do. The other thing is, he doesn't have a thirst for learning like most kids do. If you try to tell him something new, like I told him yesterday that genes are something you have in your body, he told me I was a liar. If you tell him to look at something, he will just as often turn and look the other way. I asked him the other day if he knew what *rich* meant. He responded by turning his head away, dropping his mouth open, and closing his eyes half way and moving his eyes under his lids.

It is almost impossible to correct him. For example, he was

outside watering the bushes, and I asked him to keep the hose lower because he was wetting the windows. He replied angrily, "You don't tell me what to do," and ran away. One of his biggest problems seems to be his will. It seems like, when he wants to, he can learn some seemingly difficult tasks, but most of the time, he is resistant. He'll say he's too busy, which is sort of funny, because he usually says this while he's sitting in a very relaxed position on the couch, doing nothing. Because he gets so bent out of shape when we refer to him, we sometimes try to teach him a lesson by referring to the antics of a boy we made up, called Sonny. For example, we told Arthur how Sonny was fired from a job because he yelled at a customer, after Arthur told us he was yelling, at his job, at people at the dump who were putting their garbage in the wrong place.

Arthur can read at the fourth grade level, but most of it is limited to reading signs or menus, although he has been reading TV schedules lately and car ads. He has a favorite book, that was his brother's, that he has even brought to school with him to show his teachers. It is a college spoof in cartoon form, called *I Went to College and It was Okay*. The joke of the book is that very little happens, but it is probably just this slow and simple action, or lack of it, that appeals to Arthur. He has no sense at all that this book is not a serious book. You really get a glimpse of Arthur's abilities when you see what level he picks to read or view. Most of the time, people tend to overestimate his abilities, because his vocabulary is pretty good. He uses words like *drought* and *pollution*, but most of his words are nouns that are have concrete referents. Occasionally, he will come out with something that requires some thinking. For example, he asked why, if nothing is perfect, do they have the word perfect?

Treatment

We were hoping something would be found out from doing the EEG's asleep and awake and the CAT scan, that something would be found in the brain, and we'd be able to medicate it, but [these tests] were essentially normal, so that went down the tubes. Then what are you going to do? It was stressed that we were going to have to develop a good educational program, so we called the school department and got a pre-screening. We also brought him to Worcester to check out his hearing, which was normal. Julie was always looking for things [to try]. We tried megadoses of Vitamin E and B, but he reacted really negatively. He looked like he was in pain when he urinated.

Arthur was in special classes with other kids with severe developmental disabilities, up until the ninth grade. Now he is in high school and mostly in Learning Center classes or in regular classes, like Gym or Study Careers, with an aide.

In his earlier years, he received specialized education geared more toward his needs and less toward a regular academic curriculum. For example, he spent time learning about expressions and about homonyms and homophones. He had a hard time with the difference between the words *no* and *know*. If you said, "I know," to him, which is something you said often when he was perseverating, he would say, "No, you don't know," and would become upset. Another problem he had was with the three words, *to*, *two*, and *too*. He says he hates those words and, to this day, will not eat two of anything. If he gets two meatballs in a restaurant, he has to make them into three by cutting one in half before he will start eating.

The down side of these earlier classes was [that] he was in the company of other kids who had problems that he would copy. He still says things like, "Eggies in the air, eggies are private," and "I'm going to cut off your finger," and "What about it, head," which are things he has copied from other children in his program. Now he is, for the most part, in the company of normal kids. The advantage to this is that he has more normal role models, although normal can also have its problems. He certainly has learned more swear words in these last few years.

The best part of his program now is that he has a vocational component for half of the day. So far, he has worked assembling boxes, painting, and doing outdoor work. We never thought he would be motivated to do this. It used to be almost impossible to get him to do anything when he was younger. Now he is motivated by the idea of doing things typical people do.

He is also motivated by fear. He is afraid of getting suspended at school and getting a record that might hamper his getting a job, and he is afraid of being homeless. He says he is saving his money to buy a home in Shutesbury when he is an adult. He picked that town from a map because, he said, it sounded like "shits berry." He has never been to that town and knows nothing about it. He also has no idea about the meaning of money. His grandfather once gave him a thousand dollars, and he was jumping around in glee, shouting, "Now I can buy a home in Shutesbury." We told him that he would need more than 1,000, that he needed 100,000 to buy a house, and his joy quickly turned to depression, and he was no longer happy over the gift of a thousand dollars.

He goes to a regular physician for his physical checkups, which can be pretty amusing. For example, when asked to fill up a urine cup, he did just that and brought out a specimen cup filled to the very top. He takes most things literally. He also goes to the dentist, one that is trained to work with special needs people, although, ironically, he seems very relaxed at the dentist, especially when his teeth are being cleaned. He sits in the chair with his arms up behind with neck. He has had a filling, and he did get novocaine and was pretty distressed about how his mouth felt afterwards, even though we told him it would come back to normal. He brushes his own teeth and the hygienist says he has one of the cleanest mouths she has ever seen.

Stresses on the Family

Having a child with autism has a total effect on your life. It affects everything I do. If Arthur were a normal child, you'd be looking at him having two more years of high school, then off to college, then leaving the nest while maintaining a contact. With Arthur, you don't know when, if ever, he is going to leave the house. It might not happen until he is 22. It might never happen. Everything you do is affected by the fact that you have to think of Arthur first. If you are going to go on a vacation, you're going to have to try to get the arrangements made. If I want to get involved with another project [at work], it's, can I handle this deal with Arthur? If I want to get some more schooling or go here or there, it's, what am I going to do about Arthur? When I'm home, it's, what am I going to do about Arthur? I'm always thinking about Arthur. You always think about your kids, but with a kid with autism, it's in your face all the time, and you have to constantly deal with it. So it affects your personal life, your professional life, and your home life. It makes me tired; I think it wears me down.

Cassy and I decided not to have any children, because we didn't want to risk the possibility of having a child with autism. This is something Roland will have to think about as he gets older. He very much wants children. I hope they could isolate something, so you could find out early in a pregnancy if you would have an autistic child, but they won't have that in the next ten years. I would advise my son, Roland, to work really closely with a geneticist about the whole issue, if he wants to have children.

Roland was 6 when Arthur was born. Roland was 10 when Arthur was 4 and at the point [where] we knew something was wrong, so a whole lot of energy went into Arthur. Roland was a kid who was a big ham for attention. He was cute and bright and engaging, and adults loved him. I tried to do as much as I could with Roland with sports: basketball and soccer and baseball. But I think Roland must feel that he lost a lot of his childhood to Arthur.

The hardest thing about raising Arthur is [that] it takes up too much of your time, and there's not enough for your other kids. There wasn't enough time for Roland. I think, as soon as Arthur was around, my time with Roland started getting cut in half, and then less than that and less than that. It took up too much [time to take care of Arthur], and still does take up too much.

I feel like it's a part-time job, and I don't feel like I can act naturally. I always have to think about what I'm doing, and I don't like to parent that way. I'm not the kind of person who likes to do things by a 3x5 card. But with Arthur, it's better to do things by a 3x5 card, so it's forced me to do things differently, and I don't feel real good about the way I do it.

It would be important for me to have Roland have a good relationship with Arthur as an adult. I don't mean that Roland should take Arthur into his house; that's not what I mean. I think it is important for Arthur to have someone in the world who loves him unconditionally, and I don't think there are going to be many people who do.

When Roland was 13 and Arthur 6, their mother left to live on her own. I don't think Arthur's autism had anything to do with it; we would have separated anyway. For a while, I tried to have a college student live in to watch Arthur, but I found that, rather than help, I often ended up with another person with needs to be met. Over the years, Arthur has had numerous respite workers. The ones that worked out the best were the ones who just accepted him the way he was and didn't try to educate him or change him. The ones he hated the most (the *R helpers* he calls them, because their names began with *R*) were the ones who tried to get him to stop doing something, like pinching, by pinching him back. All that did was escalate the pinching.

Long Range Forecast

The ideal would be for Arthur, someday, to live in his own apartment, with a supervisor living in the same building who would check up on him daily. At this point in time, however, there don't seem to be many facilities with this arrangement. Most facilities are group homes, which would not work out with Arthur. He refuses to sleep with anyone else. This summer, we went on vacation with my mother, and Arthur and I got an adjoining room [to hers]. But Arthur refused to sleep in the same room with anyone else and spent a good part of the night sitting up, awake, in a chair, until I thought of removing the mattress from his bed and placing it in the hallway to the bathroom.

Arthur will be getting SSI [Supplemental Security Income] when he is 18 years old, but, hopefully, he will be able to work, too. This summer, he is working without a job coach, and, so far, it is going well. I think there are a lot of jobs Arthur could have. Arthur can memorize lots of things, and he likes to do things in sequences, and when you think about it, many, many jobs are that way, for example, working at the post office. He's not going to be a regular employee, but there are spots where he could do very well. I think people just have wrong ideas, [such as,] well, we can put him in McDonald's, but McDonald's may be more difficult than lots of other jobs that may have high esteem. He can do rote sorts of things, and I think there are rote sorts of things in lots of jobs.

This is something I have to really get more involved in. I don't really know how to do that. I'm not real good at that, calling up people and trying to get jobs. But I'm going to have to do more of that. I think there are thousands of jobs Arthur could do.

Although he talks about getting married all the time, we don't think he really has a concept of marriage. I asked him if he was going to kiss his bride at the wedding; he said yes. I asked if he was going to kiss the bride after the wedding; he said he didn't know. He does know about animals and sex, but, as I said earlier, he thinks of it in terms of procreation. They are trying to initiate a program on sexuality at school, but we are telling them to go slow. If he is not interested, we don't see any need to introduce the idea to him. We're more afraid he will start using this language inappropriately as well. They are going to start talking to him about not letting other people touch him inappropriately, although I doubt that would be a problem, because he is very defensive about anyone touching him. I doubt very much he will ever get married, and that is another disappointment, like not getting a license, that he will have to deal with in the future.

Social Stigma

Now that he's in school and working with typical kids, the opportunity for harassment is more present. He told us, by writing on a piece of paper, that one of his fellow students told him he was going to cut off his peepee. Without being there, though, it's hard to know how much Arthur starts himself. He says kids in the hall spit on his neck. Again, spitting is something Arthur would do, so it is hard to tell if he is projecting, or if he is spitting first and the kids are responding in kind, or if they are really doing this to him without provocation. He has also had a few episodes of kids getting him to give them money. It wasn't difficult; Arthur said he didn't know how to say no.

All the other times he is out, he is in our company, so he is protected from harassment, although, one time, we were getting gas, and he was mocked. Arthur always jumps out of the car to wash off the windshield whenever we stop for gas. This time some of his school mates were at the next pump and saw him and started to imitate his movements. They didn't see that I was watching. When they did, they drove off, fortunately. I was ready to go after them.

When Arthur was younger, he would get lots of people staring at him and us. Because he looked so normal, I think, people weren't sure if he was just a normal kid being bad, who had lousy parents who weren't disciplining him, or a kid with problems. Now, because of his size, it is more obvious that something is wrong with him, and people are less likely to stare.

Surviving and Transcending

When things are going well, I can talk with Arthur, I can converse with him. He can read, he has some fun every once in a while. He has a kind of a sense of humor. And those are all things I didn't ever know if he was going to experience. There was a time where I didn't know if things were going to get worse or he was going to have to be institutionalized. I look at all the good things that have happened to him. I mean, he's come an incredible way. I don't know what percentage of that success I'm a part of, but, from where he was as a young child to where he is now, it certainly far exceeds what most professionals told me, and it exceeds what I thought would happen. He's much more of a human being than I thought he would be, so that's really positive. He's got a summer job now, and he's basically doing it, with lots of help, I'm sure, but he's acting normal in many ways.

You have to constantly look at [the situation as though] the glass is half full, all the time. Otherwise, you could get very depressed. And I take real pride and joy in the things that Arthur can accomplish. I really feel it when he does something right.

The best advice I can give to other parents is, first, get into the best educational program you can get in. If your goal is to get him to be the best that he can be, you have to quickly get him involved in an educational program that you're happy with and establish a cooperative, working relationship with his teachers. I've seen families get advocates and get into adversarial relationships with their kid's teachers, and they may win the battle, but they've lost the war.

And get all the support you can. Some people do well in groups. I don't feel like I have the time or the energy or the desire to be with a group. That's not what makes me feel better, but for some people, that may be a good idea. You have to find, at least, a few people to talk to who will be honest with you. You don't want someone saying, "Oh, everything is going to be all right," and you don't want someone constantly saying you should put the kid into an institution. You've got to find someone who is in between there, who is going to be supportive of you at times and critical of you at other times.

Chapter 5
The Farmer

This is the story of David, a 16-year-old boy with autism, as recounted by his foster mother, Jane, with permission from his biological father. David lives with his foster mother and father, his foster brother, Ned, who is 12, and his foster sister, Missy, who is 8. Over the last few years, the family has also had an exchange student and a friend living with them. David became a foster child in this family when he was five years old. Jane is a speech and language specialist, and her husband is a self-employed carpenter.

First Meeting

[When we were first looking into fostering David,] we were told that he was very difficult to manage at home and he was disconnected. His teacher at the time [told us he was autistic,] but it wasn't in the records. But we went to his class and observed him in school and talked to his parents.

The whole class was [made up of] really cute kids. Then we saw David. We knew he was going to be very difficult, but we were pretty sure we could manage him, because we've had a lot of training. We had training together, [in Europe,] working with kids like him, so we were pretty sure we could present a united front. [At that time, our son,] Ned, was one[-year-old].

Our hope [was that it would be a permanent foster arrangement]. We liked the fact that he had a natural family, because they still had primary responsibility. We liked the idea of sharing him. He still goes once a month for a weekend to his Dad's.

Cause

I don't know all the details [of what caused David to become autistic]. One of his brothers or sisters has a lot of physical problems. One of his brothers is very small. He's been in special education for quite awhile. A lot of her kids were premature. In fact, David was the only one that wasn't premature. He was post date. And his Mom's quite small physically and was a smoker. I don't know if

that [contributed]. And he did get an infection after he was born. I
don't know what it was from, but he was hospitalized.

Grief and Sorrow

[His biological parents] were having marital problems. They had 5
other children. He was the fifth. One of the children [needed lots of
medical attention]. They were just completely overwhelmed.

[David] wouldn't sleep, wouldn't eat, [he was] up all night,
and they had no support services. When we got him, he had basically never been to a grocery store, never been out of the yard.
He'd been to some program and back, but he'd hadn't had any
experiences. They couldn't manage, and they were heartbroken to
do this.

I think it was suggested to them at one point, by the state, to
put David in foster care, and then they thought about it. They
thought that maybe their problems would ease up when he was out
of the house. But they did get divorced, maybe a couple of years
after. They have joint custody, but [the father] has physical custody. David's Dad's been really helpful and respectful, so we have
a lot of support from him.

We could tell [at the time we first saw him] that he had autism
[and we knew what autism entailed]. I [just] thought he would
relate a little bit more, eventually. Looking back now, I really wish
we had somebody who was more retarded, who could really bond
more with the kids.

[With our family and friends,] I think there was some sense of,
why are you doing this? why do you want to do it? mostly——they
couldn't believe it; they could not believe it——-and, why bother?
That came later.

Day-to-Day Living

He has a long history of sleep problems, and he usually doesn't go
to sleep until the last person is settled in the house. We keep a very
strict routine at bedtime, and he knows, for example, he can't sit
up, because he would sit up all night. So we've done behavioral
things to get him to lay down. We've done stuff, like stand outside

his door and go in and lay him down, like in the early years, over and over and over again.

We've done stuff, like, if you get up I will take your quilt away, his special quilt, and that worked for a really long time. The if-and-then [approach], that's worked for the last two years, but before that, using that stuff didn't work.

And now he's at the point [where] he goes right in. He used to laugh and make noises, and we don't allow that. [We say to him,] "You're going to sleep, go be quiet." We talk to him a lot. We set the stage for what a normal person would do, and force him into it, and it works.

I did have to stay up most of the night a few nights, the very first nights he ever came. We weren't [tolerating this], 'cause we knew that was the worst problem his parents had. He adapted very quickly with that. We get our way. We win the fights. It's our family we're protecting.

I think a lot of people give up. They just give up. My philosophy is: just keep doing it. I would do something three, four hundred times. I'm not exaggerating. And I don't give up, because it doesn't help. The key has been persistence, not patience, persistence, like, you're strong, but I'm stronger; and we're still battling about a lot of things.

He used to dress himself. We're in a regression right now. We would put the clothes out for him, and he would get dressed, and he would come down, but now he just sits. It took us at least 5 or 6 years to get him to dress himself. He had no motivation. What worked is, I remember, I sat him down, took his pajamas off, and then I'd go out, and I'd call him. I'd say, "David, come on let's go," and he'd come out, and he knew that was wrong. But when I insisted he come and I knew he wasn't ready, that was wrong to him. It was like, wait a minute, I'm supposed to have my clothes. So then he would go back. That's pretty much how we got him to dress. He was completely able to dress himself, and he would dress himself, I think, almost every time. The problem is [that] his sense of time passage is not there. He might, conceivably, wait half an hour before putting the first thing on. To get him to dress at the normal pace, you have to use continual prompting.

It's very frustrating, when you say, "Get your shoes, it's time to go," and he just sits with his shoes. He gets them, then he sits. And then you have to say, "Put your shoes on." He can do it; it just doesn't occur to him. He will pick dirty clothes out of the laundry basket to put on. If I leave him, he will get dressed in the same thing as yesterday.

Everything is ritualized; we're pretty firm. We've seen that this is the path to a healthy individual, so we know we're right. Other people find it very controlling. People that don't understand that, in two days, he could be hitting you in the face, because you won't let him get the dirty shirt out of the laundry. He goes from normal-like behaviors to extremely obsessive behavior in seconds. So they don't understand why we're doing it. If you give him an inch, he keeps going in that direction.

For example, we used to have a quilt around his neck for comfort. Then he had to have two, then he had to have it tied a certain way, and he had to have it tied a better way, and he would unknot it, and that was it, finished. When he can control himself, he can get it. We don't let his obsessions rule him, [at least] we try not to.

[We] help him shower. He'd wash the same spot over and over. He won't move around the body. He'd be fine if he had a bath every night, or twice a day, if you wanted him to. He likes the bath. He dries himself now. He will dry himself pretty well, which is a new skill. If you wash his face, or if he washes his face, he'll say, "Dry," because he doesn't like the feeling. It's a good awareness, which is really fantastic.

He can brush his teeth pretty well, but [with] his hair, he combs the same spot. He's disconnected. He doesn't connect [that] this is his hand. He doesn't integrate, like, I have a job to do and this is how I'm going to do it. He doesn't know why he's doing it.

We used to have big huge fights [about cutting his hair]. He would reach with both hands and grab and scream, but now he's good, but I still have to be right with him, because he will put his hand up. I have him get a good haircut, and then I do it for about 4 months. He doesn't like his ears touched and his neck. And cutting nails used to be horrendous. I think that was the worst: nails and toenails. It would take two of us to hold him down, and now I can do it alone. I'd like to teach him to do it.

Now he pretty much eats regularly, but he'll try to refuse foods, and he'll also hold the fork like a baby, and he'll, like, try to drink and not eat. It'll get on his lips, and he'll drool and not lick his lips and spill, but with just a few cues at the right time, he can eat very nicely. He used to stuff and not swallow, and then he would swallow so quickly and not chew.

We've been pretty strict. This is what we're having, this is what you eat, and we've been very strict, and he basically eats everything. He doesn't like textures. He likes baby food, macaroni, something soft. And he eats everything now, but he resists textures. What helps is barbecue sauce [on meat], then he can slurp it down.

We've had lots of battles over this. He's very, very badly food obsessed. He just has to have it, wants it, thinks about it, asks for it when he comes in, doesn't know when he's full.

He follows us around, especially right now. If we walk out, he'll follow us. He's afraid he's going to hurt himself, so he wants us near him, because he knows we won't let him. He's self-abusive and if he gets nervous, he starts to pinch himself and bite himself. He'll ask for help.

He's gone through every phase of [self-abuse], and we had a few years where he really didn't do it at all at home, but he did it a lot at school. And now he does it, sort of, whenever he gets anxious. He does a lot of fake abuse, fake biting, fake pinching. He goes into postures. He'll have his hands up behind his back and you'll think, oh, he's trying not to bite himself, but it's a start of a bite, so we keep his hands down. It's been years and years and years of work on this.

We tied his sweatshirt and he had gloves, all things he could take off, pretty much. He had them so he couldn't bite his wrists. It helped him, [but] he got very dependent on them very quickly. Then he had to have it; you couldn't get it off him.

[They did it], mostly, at school. He had a padded sweatshirt at school for about eight or nine months. They couldn't get it off, and he'd come home and just hang it up on the door, every day. And we'd hide it, and he'd go find it. That was one of the more creative things he's ever done: go hunt for something.

He does quite a bit [around the house]. He sets the table, and he helps with preparing meals, and he's helped to carry firewood for us for years and years, and he delivers laundry around the house. He dries the dishes beautifully. He wipes, he sweeps. One of our philosophies is that he has to be helpful, that he has to contribute, and he's really helpful. He'll put things away. He knows where things belong and offers to put things away. Just spontaneously, he'll walk by and see something out and put it in the cupboard where it belongs. It keeps him busy, [and] it gives us free time. So I can say, "Get the paper," and he'll go get the paper, [but] he'll say no every time. In fact, you can see me do it [now].

[*Jane speaks to David:*] David, get up, get your shoes, and you're going to get the paper and bring it here. Put the flag down, remember, I showed you. Go on, and you can put the flag down.

[*Jane speaks to the interviewer:*] We get a "no" to everything, which is another problem.

[*To David:*] Go on David, get going, get your shoes and go get the paper. No, get your shoes, David, get your shoes.

[*To the interviewer:*] But when he gets it, he's really happy that he's done it. I have a theory that he's obsessing about something, like it's time for supper, or they're not in the kitchen, or I want that pudding on the shelf. And when I break [into his obsession] with a command, a request, he's somewhere else, he's on his own thing. He could be thinking about pudding, and I'll offer him a cookie, which is his favorite thing, and he'll reject it, because he's stuck. So that's why I think he says no.

He's like, dangling in space. It's like, what is it, what is it, where am I? Then once you get him going, he's fine. He'll say, "No walk," and two seconds later, he's laughing, he's relaxed, he's hiking, but most people hear the no and they panic. [They think] he doesn't want to. You can't assume he doesn't want to. We have to assume, we have to judge, it's healthy for you to help, it's healthy for you to walk. We make those judgments, we don't let him, because, otherwise, he'd just be on the sofa.

[*To David:*] Put your shoes on, David. Don't sit down. [*To the interviewer:*] When he sits down, he just stops. [*To David:*] Don't sit down, put your shoe on, get the paper. [*To the interviewer:*] He's in this new phase where he doesn't initiate, so I have to keep on him. [*To David*:] Keep going, no stopping. [*To the interviewer*:] I'm trying a new cue: no stopping. [*To David*:] Put your shoe on, David. Put your shoe on and get the paper please. Good boy. Okay, no coat, no coat. [*To the interviewer*:] He turned the light out.

[*To David*:] Okay, you're going to get the paper with two hands, and you're going to put the flag down. Remember, I showed you. So out you go, and then you come back in, and we'll get ready for supper. Okay, close the door, you don't have to open it up that wide.

[*To the interviewer*:] His hands are full of mail, but he hasn't got the paper. So I'll have him go back out. Hang on a second, I'll be right back. I have to always check to see that he's following through. You know, we only force him if we think it's for his own good, but, I mean, I'm sure there would be some people who think, well, why do you make him? They would just as soon leave him alone or something, think he would be happier with that, and you know what that would result in.

Oh, God, he doesn't understand. [*To David*:] David, what did you find? What did you find? [*To the interviewer*:] I don't know what he's found. He just doesn't comprehend. Okay, I'm just going to watch. [*To David*:] Good boy, keep going.

[*To the interviewer*:] People don't understand, they're always saying [to him], "How old are you?" They have no idea that he has no understanding. I mean, there's just so much he doesn't understand conceptually. He understands so much less than what you think.

He just put the flag down. I mean, he would never ever have done that, even a year ago. He would never have scanned, gone back, figured out the problem. He would never have even begun, and that's really a very big step for him. [*To David*:] Thank you, David. Thank you."

[His birthday is coming up.] We usually wrap up peanut butter cups and pudding: things he likes. He has no concept, really. We have a party, and we have the cake, and he blows it out, and we make a big fuss. He enjoys the moment, but he doesn't say, like, it's my birthday. He opens the presents, and we try to give him things that are age appropriate. We don't like anything that is babyish. We gave him those spiritual balls with the bells in them. They're metal balls; I think you roll them. We gave him a [big] red ball [that he can sit and bounce on]. We give him things he can use. We try to keep it appropriate, which is very hard. We give him clothes, his parents send presents, but for years, he wouldn't even really open [them], but he will open them [now].

He talks. He knows all the words for everything, single words. He puts some concepts together. He'll request, he'll deny, he'll tell some things about the cat, and he'll talk about the future. He can sequence. I can say, "We're going to the mall, then we're going to a restaurant, then we're going roller skating, and then we're coming home, and you're going to have a snack," and he can hold all that in his memory. He can follow, and he asks for a massage and to go swimming. It's mostly requests. He never calls [your name]. He doesn't call anybody anything ever.

He says, "Help." We've been working on that for seven years, for 5,000 times, and now he says, "Help." He'll say, "Gloves, car, coat, go toilet, I want pudding." He's really improving all the time. He says, "Hi," he says, "No bye bye, no bye bye," meaning he doesn't want to go with you, but he's very aware now. He never would have had this conversation a year ago. He would have been saying, "No farm, no bite, no pinch." He would have been eavesdropping. He'd hear it and think it was happening right now. He'd say, "Don't wet the bed and interrupt." His new words are *I'm tired, I'm tired of that, I'm tired of it.* I guess it's what I say all the time. It's the truth, I am tired.

People would say, don't say no, because he'll [have a] temper [tantrum]. You know, [you're supposed to walk on] egg shells. Don't say yogurt, because, if he doesn't get it, he's going to hit. So we kept saying milk, yogurt, pudding, cookies, Twinkies, over and over. He thought it was funny. We used humor. We'd go right after the obsession. He has an elevator obsession. He wants the elevator. They like the doors. Autistic people like automatic things, things like the waves, over and over, that are predictable. You want the elevator, there it is. We're not going on it right now. I'm sorry. Anything that's obsessive, we don't get fearful around him, we have no fear, and most people are very fearful. Don't say the word elevator or he'll be up all night, you know. We just say it. It's really fun, so we never avoided it. We try to get it out in the open so he can clear it up. We're not afraid of David, but lots of people are afraid.

He seems to be [affectionate]. I think a lot of people wouldn't interpret it as affectionate, but, when you see the pattern over a long period of time, you get the idea. He doesn't demonstrate affection in a normal way; he won't come up [to you]. He likes physical contact, and he likes to be tickled. He puts his head at you, you know like the Rainman. He loves his shoulders rubbed. Look, he's laughing. He's quite affectionate. He loves coming in the big bed with all the family; he loves to cuddle up under the covers.

There are problems, [however,] with masturbating in public. He's gotten himself very aroused in really inappropriate situations and stuff, [though] we really haven't had problems with it. Other people have pretended to ignore it, [but] you can't ignore him. He doesn't have a sense of where he is and what's appropriate and what's inappropriate. [Once or twice] he'll lie on his stomach on the floor and roll around, which we don't allow. We've gotten him out of that. [We] stop it in inappropriate places, and then leave him in his own room. That's something that we respect, their privacy. But we make it very clear that you're not doing it in public. He can't even go on the floor. [We tell him,] you don't lay on the floor.

He has been doing it in school. I've seen him sexually aroused and laying on the floor. It's ridiculous, you know, and the teachers are ignoring or pretending to ignore it. You have to be pretty dense and unaware to not know what is going on.

He [also] has a lot of fears. He has this strange thing about heights: he's afraid of them and is fascinated by them. If he sees a ladder, he'll ask to climb up it.

[Another thing that is unusual is that] he twiddles. Any thread, he'll pick it up, and he'll twiddle, separate the [threads]. Move it like this, roll it. He's done everything, [including] hyperventilate. He's done everything, [including] rock. We just try to stop and redirect.

[Also,] he's very uncoordinated. He has a limited range of

motion, with his arms and also with his back, bending. He holds himself in such a limited position. He walks very erect and very balanced and takes very short steps, for him, and he keeps his elbows close to his body at all times. He can't put his hands straight up in the air, he's physically unable. Because he's kept himself for so long like that, he's actually lost the range of motion. He can't easily bring his knee up to his chest. He couldn't even walk when we got him. He would see a pine needle and think it was like a cliff. He's really good now; we walk hundreds of miles with him. We make him walk, run, ride a bike. He skates. Basically it's a love-hate [relationship]. It's "no, no," and yet, if you don't take him skating, he's crying, "Skate, skate." But see, that looks like [a] human rights issue, you're forcing him.

The school has physical therapists come in, speech therapists, every kind of specialist. He also has undeveloped fine motor coordination with his hands. Like you saw with the fork, he just grabs the whole thing. He is really physically handicapped. It's an emotional thing that's led up to this. He can't jump, and he doesn't skip, he just barely walks. [But you said you took him roller skating?] We do. We do everything with him. He doesn't know how to do it, but he's on the skates, trying.

He can hurt himself and, literally, have a delayed reaction of a full minute, or two minutes, before he realizes that he's in pain. I want to teach him to do the hot and cold water. He knows hot and cold, but he doesn't really think. And the reason I'm so excited about him asking for his face to be dry [is] because he could have a mosquito sticking out of his face sucking the blood and he won't swat them. He'll sit there with flies on his face or mosquitoes on his face and not move. And so, the fact that he knows that his face is wet is a start. This is a big deal. A little thing like that, for us, is a major breakthrough.

The other night I said, "Do your breathing," [for relaxation,] and we haven't done it in, like, three years, and he did 10 breaths by himself. Usually, he just stops, and he kept going 10 times, which is a major thing for him. He's just learning, he's still learning, and we're still fighting.

We have lots of pets, and he doesn't really give them much

attention. We force him to pet the bunny, pet the cow, [but he has] no interest really. We put pets on him. We put rats on his shoulder; we do it on purpose. He says, "Off, off, off." We keep him involved; we don't like dead time.

[Another problem is] he has no [sense of] safety in the road. He would go right in front of a car. I've tried it. I've gone right in front of him and honked the horn, and he doesn't look.

[But] we take him to the Cape, [on vacation,] and he loves the ocean. And he sleeps in the tent, he loves the tent. He sleeps by himself, and sometimes he sleeps with us too. But when you're in public, he's always got to be right with you.

The good thing is, you can say, "David, go to your room," and he's gone for a good two hours. He will sit. He doesn't drain us regularly. It's when he's in a bad state [that] we all get tense.

But I can say, "David go out." We have a hammock, we have all kinds of things, and he'll go on the hammock, which I think is appropriate. He'll be gone for two hours. Or [he'll play] on the [big red] ball. He can occupy himself. He's very nice. Don't you think he's nice?

I [just] wish that he was more bonded. I know he likes us, but is it us or is it just because we take care of his needs?

But here's a harsh point: We really like David, but when he's gone, we do not miss him. We don't miss him. When he's back, we're happy to see him (and I think I talk very bluntly, but it's after years of this arrangement), [but] this is the hard reality, 'cause I adore David: I like him a lot, I really think he's really functionally helpful, but when he's gone, I don't even think about him.

Treatment

He has medicine; it's Haldol. It's for helping him sequence in his mind, so that he can follow through better, but it did help him sleep, as well. [He's been on Haldol] for 4 years or more. [It's also for his Tourette's syndrome.] Without it, he'll have facial tics.

We have started facilitated communication, and believe it or not, he does do some of it, on a basic level. They do it at school; I do a little here. We've been doing it about a month. We'll say, "What do you do at the farm?" He does type. We didn't think he knew any letters at all, I have to confess this. And he will type *shovel*. Apparently, he answers questions, but what I found is that, if I have any idea what the answer is, I strongly influence him. And it's like, 20% him and 80% me, and they say, at school, they've done it without looking, which doesn't fit the philosophy, because, apparently, you're supposed to look and correct errors, and they say he does it. And I've asked them things, like ask David what our new pet is or who he had supper with, and it's been totally false both times with them, and they just sort of justify it. And I feel that a yes-no [question] has a 50% chance. [If he gets it wrong], they just say, well, you know, he had a bad day or he was silly. And they said once, "How do you feel about your communication?", and he said *insecure*. I just don't believe he has those concepts. I do not believe it.

It's very, very hard, as a parent or whatever I am to him, to have them tell me that they know more about my kid and that I've missed this big thing. Our philosophy has been, can you function in today's society? And if it helps him, fine, but his behavior has just gone down hill, if anything, and I am very strongly reality based.

At 2 o'clock, they're finished; no one has ever called David. No one has ever invited him over socially in his whole life. They've only taken him if they were paid. And so, to pretend that you have a relationship with him infuriates me. We have the real relationship. We sweat, we cry, you know, we fight, we stick by David, we battle for him, and they tell me he's insecure about his communication! And I'm a communication specialist by career. But it's very much us-against-them. We try not to, but it's like [they ask us,] "Have you typed lately?" And, you know, [they say,] "With us, he has answered perfectly."

They took David down to one of the workshops, and they claimed he said yes [to the question], "Do you want to keep this conversation private?" So there we are, 25 people, and he's, like, keeping these secret answers. [They ask him,] "David, where do you live?" *Great Barrington.* "Great, that's really good." [He doesn't live in Great Barrington.] "David, how old are you? *14.* He's 15. "David, do you like Coke?" *Yes.* He doesn't. It's like, come off it, and they had the nerve to say David's typing sentences! And the whole room believed it, except for me and his respite worker, who transported him there for me.

So I'm taking it slowly, with an open mind overall, but even if he types, what's the heart of [his] reality? [One boy we heard of] types these essays. Wonderful. He wants friends. What does he do on the bus? Screams, yells, hits, masturbates! He can't even control himself for half an hour! [If] you can't control yourself for half and hour, you're nowhere.

I don't care if you can type essays about your Italian friend who's autistic. Let's get real! So even if he does it, I'm not impressed. Because I'm impressed with behavior that's social, and I'm not going to sit in a room when David's snotty, kicking me, hitting me, laying on the floor masturbating. I mean, I'm not going to do it.

They've been disrespectful to me and my work of 12 years with this boy, [just] because honestly, I swear to God, when I'm typing with him, I honestly can not tell if I'm doing it for him. [It's hard to tell,] because you just have to look at the letters, and its pretty easy to hit them, and if you don't look, he'll just do the same thing over and over.

The problem is [that] I want to be able to say, "David, go to the kitchen and get me two spoons; we need two more." When they get out their computer and they say he [types], well, who the hell cares? If you can't do it personally, don't do it. I don't want the computers. I want him to be able to set the table. [I want him to be able to look at a piece of clothing and say,] "This is dirty, I'm going to put it in the laundry." This is what I beg them to do: functional [behavior training]. What are you doing? Is this important? Does he need to do it? And they don't know how to teach it. They have no idea how to teach it.

I just trained this worker at the YMCA. I went five times, on my Friday off, to show him how to use the [exercise] machines. It's really easy. [I showed him how to help David:] "You pull it up to your chest, David. Chest, pull it back. Okay, another one." So I go in the other week, and I just happened to walk by, and I forgot David was there. I was swimming, and there he is, and the worker's behind him, and David's just sitting there. He's not doing it, and the guy's just sort of looking away. I said, "What are you doing?" He said, "Well, he [couldn't do it]." I said, "Well, so what? David, lift it up. Okay, pull it back." You do that a couple hundred times, and he's got it for the rest of his life. I really advocate for David. I really want him to be all he can be, but I have no luck with the general population. They don't have the drive.

If I try and teach David and it doesn't work, I automatically think, well, how can we do it better next time? I never think, oh, he can't do it. It's like, this isn't working. Like sitting up in bed, I try something, and then I think, well, that doesn't work, what else can I do?

He was real aggressive all last year in school. [He hurt people lots of times.] Hits, head butts, tearing glasses off bus drivers, kicks, really big kicks. And I went and met with them. It took about a year and a half, because they have to go through a trial. The message was, it's okay to hit in school 10-15 times a day, so I said, "You just tell him that if he hits, he's going to walk," because we walk for therapy with him a lot. And it has to be fast, quick, dramatic, and short. It could be one minute, and you do that, and then the next time he starts to hit, you just tell him, "David, want to go for a fast walk?", and he says, "No." So they did it, and it worked. This is after many, many, many years of severe aggression and self-abuse. And they did it, and it went from 10 hits down to 1, and then it went down to a fake, and now he doesn't hit any more.

But there was this human rights issue: You're making him walk faster than he wants to walk. [But] he's more dignified now. The school was willing to do it, but I know the next program won't do it.

He spent almost a whole year on a mat in one class, just vegetating. I know how to keep him healthy, and walking does relax him. The positive [reinforcers] don't work. What's aversive to one is not aversive to another. It was dramatic—I prefer to call it dramatic. It was very clear.

We can see antecedents [to violent behavior], little gestures, and we just say, "Don't you dare. If you do, I'll put you straight to bed," or something like that. These behaviors are all still there, you know, but he's much happier when he's under control. The psychologist always says to us, well why can't he have self control? Well, I'd love him to, and he does to a certain extent, but, I mean, I'm not going to sit around and wait while he hits me a couple of hundred times.

We're very assertive, and I can't imagine how it is with people who are not highly educated and assertive. I've spent hundreds of hours on the phone on this kid. I can tell you, this week alone, I've met with teachers, I've had 4 or 5 phone calls about the farm [that we hope he will live at someday], and I've called a psychologist about a new program.

Stresses on the Family

When he goes away to respite or to camp, he's up all night. He sits up, he won't get in bed, he laughs, he puts the light up and down. We have programs that we give them, but they don't follow them. [They say,] "We thought if he was in his room, it would be okay." [He's] up all night, then he sleeps all the next day; he reverses day and night.

After [his last] respite, [he came back with] just thousands of bruises all over his body, flesh torn up, infected wounds [on his] neck, wrists. He had to go to the hospital emergency room and [get] antibiotics. He had secondary infections where his whole hand puffed up.

It's very depressing, and he gets paralyzed with fear when he's self-abusing and he's waiting for some controls, [but] they don't follow through. We have hundreds of pages of detailed instructions. Like, here's a really bad one. One of the rules is, you get him up around 8; you don't have to get him out of bed, but you wake him up. So I left a friend to go pick him up at respite, and he's sound asleep at noon. Well, where's breakfast? He's underweight. They said, "It's vacation." Well, it's not vacation. Then he's up there the whole next night in pain.

The self-abuse is really intense, but he knows we won't allow it. I'll tell him to get out of the house, and that works sometimes, or [we'll] put him to bed if he's really nervous. The thing with the self-abuse is, when he does it, it's a very direct communication. He looks right at you, and he tries to affect his environment, and it's very frightening. He knows we won't tolerate it, he knows [he's in] big trouble [if he does it]. I'm mean, it's disgusting to watch.

We find that experience [of respite workers] means nothing. It's more the personality, if the person's strong, caring, and assertive. Because, if you have a sort of apathetic, I-don't-care-it's-okay [attitude], then he freaks out. We've had lots of ads in the paper. We've used every resource you can imagine. We have [respite] for an hour a day, a weekend, three-day weekends, a week, two weeks, everything you can imagine.

[The last time, when he was self-abusing,] they didn't do anything. They just allowed it to happen. They said they didn't realize. The usual [excuse] is, they say they didn't see him do it. Well, they're being paid to see him do it! They always try to blame somebody else, and we have a whole program now where they have to call a social worker if there's [a problem].

He can do a lot of damage to himself in a very short amount of time. It would be possible for someone to not realize what a state he's in and just leave him for half an hour or hour and not realize. He looks fairly calm. [For example, he will] have a coat on and he will have bitten and he will refuse to take it off. He won't take it off, so then it will get infected.

The quality of respite care is so bad. They get paid so much to do it, and they don't follow through. They don't maintain even the basic standard of care. We've had big meetings this year, and we basically told them, you are getting him quality respite or we're not going to have him in the family. Because it's terrible for him to go and get into this panic, and it's their job to see that he's safe: that he's fed, clothed, and safe from himself.

[Some of his worst respites have been in controlled environments.] He's been to [a facility] in Boston with round-the-clock staffing and nursing and come back the worst that he's ever been: completely and utterly bloody. The people that succeed are the ones that are strong-willed. Like, you're not doing that to me. That type of personality is effective immediately. Like, cut it, but most people want to try their own thing, like, it's okay, you don't have to eat, you don't have to go to bed. Then he self-starves. He becomes so out of himself.

It's very frustrating, and it's embarrassing, and it's so draining,

[but] we're trying so hard to make this model work. I've talked to [people in] specialized home care, and they feel the family model is the best, but you wonder sometimes, when he comes back from respite. The next time he comes home with broken skin, I'm going to file for child abuse, because they're not taking care of my kid. We're going to Bermuda, and we're going for seven days, with my family and my brother's family, and I've told the social worker, "If I come back from Bermuda, and he's bitten up and overtired, I'm not taking him back." They can get him back to the way he was when I left him.

We've always [only] asked for maintenance, we've asked for just the baseline care, no training, no recreation. We've asked that he's fed, that he sleeps, and that he doesn't hurt himself. A dog gets better care than David! And [the social worker] can't [deliver it]. She just doesn't follow through. She has to make sure, that's her job, and she doesn't do it. It's very, very stressful.

Well, we just had the big confrontation. For years, we just managed and troubleshooted, and we finally had this big meeting, and she keeps coming to us, [asking,] "What do you want me to do?" She keeps trying to get us to tell her how to do her job. It's her job, you figure it out. She says, "You want me to call every day?" It's her problem. Your job is to keep my kid safe. I told her, "I have enough to do, I can't do everything." I said, "You do the respite," and I said, "From now on, as far as I'm concerned, I'm giving you the dates, and we're out of here on those dates." She's still calling me. She says, "Well who do you want to take him?" I don't care. These are the dates, do your job. [She wants] me to call, me to transport, me to train the people, me to evaluate, me to troubleshoot.

Long Range Forecast

We're trying to get him onto a farm. There's a Camphill Village, in New York, and these are all over the world. It's a farming community, and no one is paid, nobody, [not even] staff or doctors, and it's a self-sufficient farm. They do everything by hand; they milk the cows by hand. We met in a place like this, in [Europe]. They believe that the handicapped person is passing through this lifetime in a sort of defective body, so they try to address the soul. They believe in reincarnation (I'm not saying I do), and they teach, and they do lots and lots of music, exercise, and dance. They have a cultural life; they have concerts. It's like a family. [They have] anywhere from 4 to 8 or 10 villagers, and there's co-workers from around the world that come and volunteer. And they make crafts, they have a book bindery. I mean real crafts. They make real candles. It's quality stuff. They're serious, competitive, expensive, you know, silk shawls, and I want him to go there. I don't know if he can get in. They take people depending on what they need to balance each house out. It starts at age 22. I want him to go there; that's our plan. I want him in a physical job, because physical work relaxes him. I don't want him standing in a workshop. He has too much nervous energy.

It is a 780-acre farm with 200 villagers, but there's other smaller ones. Our whole time has been focused on giving him the training, 'cause he's going to go with skills. He has lots of skills. But he's going to have to dress himself, and he has to have [a sense of] self-preservation to go there. He goes to a farm three or four mornings a week now, and he's very resistant, because they haven't done the battles. See, you battle him once, like, you're going to carry this bucket, and [then] he's going to carry it forever.

We hope he goes there; we think it's a very rich life there. It's very rich and healthy, and it's what we want for him. Their idea is that everybody has a contribution to make, and we jolly well better do it, you know. And it's very dignified. Everyone's dressed up, and there's a very strict routine, and it works for a certain kind [of handicapped person]. The higher level ones want to be out [in the mainstream of life], and lower level ones would need too much physical care. So he's a perfect candidate, 'cause he doesn't need that physical care and he doesn't care if he's out in the world.

Social Stigma

People mostly just stare. I think it's like, why are you making him do that? or don't make him do it. They pretty much leave us alone. Some people come and try to help him. [They ask me,] "Why are you carrying your son? Why don't you just give him the candy?

Why don't you just let [him do whatever he's doing]?" [But] it's emotional blackmail: if he knows he can do it, he'll do it, so it's really embarrassing. I'm very embarrassed to take David out. I am.

I know everybody in [this town]. I work in the schools. He'll start laughing in the store as loud as he can, and then he'll start clapping, over and over. Drives me nuts. We used to take him everywhere, for years, and now we're more and more [using the approach]: you want to stay in the car or want to come in?

The other day, I took him folk dancing. I only wanted to go for half an hour—it was a little church thing—and we told him to sit on the stage, and he was pinching. I can't even folk dance for 20 minutes, and he was posturing. Come off [it]. I mean, he used to sit, and he used to listen. And he's bribing us now: If you don't sit next to me, I'm going to do this to you. And we can't get that heavy in front of everybody.

Surviving and Transcending

Most of the time I like [having David around], but when he's tense, I can't keep calm, because he carries the tension [to me], so I always work at keeping him calm. Because we get a lot of respite, it works, but it's hard, it's frustrating, but then he does some stupid thing, like breathing 10 times, that will keep me going, I swear, for months.

Or he'll use some new little skill. He'll say some new thing that he's never said before, and those [achievements] carry me. He'll do some new trick, like put the flag down, and all I need are those every few months. It's amazing, such a stupid little thing, and it's like, oh, my God, I can't believe he said that, I can't believe he did that. I'll say, "I really like you, you really did a good job," like with the mail.

[My husband and I] are very honest with David. We're brutally honest with him. We don't do any pretending. If he's not doing something right, [we let him know], and I think that's respectful. We don't ever pretend with him.

We have respite for our support, and we talk to his Dad, and we talk to his social worker, which is not that supportive, and we do a lot of physical exercise, and we go on vacations all the time.

We just do it. We don't wait. We go to Bermuda, from here to California. We go camping.

And we talk a lot, too much, about David. We talk about him all the time. We have to stop. It's boring for the kids. We don't go to support groups now, because we just don't have time. We take Spanish, we always study, so we're studying, we're exercising, we just don't have time. We work hard to take care of ourselves [and] we really believe in what we're doing.

I would advise someone with a child with autism to get all the help you can, right away. Get respite right away. Make it a part of your life. Get a functional communications advocate, get some-body who's going to help your child communicate effectively, and get lots of breaks. And talk to lots of other parents. And get your kid mainstreamed. I believe it really helps. Be realistic. Don't give up.

It's the worst disability to have. There's nothing worse. [It's] much better to be blind or deaf or anything but this. This is not a way to be in the world. It's a combination of so many different things. He's got everything, but we're hanging in. We're pretty per-severant people, because I believe everybody has a purpose, and I'm sorry he's autistic, but you know, we have to get on with it.

Chapter 6
The Linebacker

 This is the story of James, a 19-year-old boy who lives at home with his mother and father. He has an older brother, Robert, who had been living away at college, but is now home while he plans his graduate education. The interview was with James's mother, Eleanor. I met Eleanor after hours at her place of business, a busy flower shop on a main street. She has left teaching and has been working here a few years. Her husband is a coach at a local college.

Diagnosis

James was my second child. Robert, [my first child,] was an extremely easy child to raise, [so] I just assumed that James would be the same. There's nobody on [either] my side of the family or my husband's, going back two to three generations, [that] had a major disability. My pregnancy with James was extremely easy. I knew what to expect; everything went right along on schedule. I didn't even feel pregnant most of the time. The whole time I was pregnant, I never took an aspirin, never drank, [and] I don't smoke. I had no medication during delivery, until they forced it on me at the very end. They gave me a spinal, but I really didn't need it. The labor was easy, even though it was long. [But] when James came home from the hospital, the first six to nine months that he was with us as a newborn, I just didn't feel you could cuddle him. He just didn't react the way Robert had. When I would go to the pediatrician and mention something, he would say, "Well, every baby is different." And I said, "Well, you know he just doesn't seem the same, he doesn't feel the same," And he said, "Give him time. He's his own little person." [But] by the time he was a year old, he was just not relaxed when you cuddled him, and it didn't matter who it was, anybody. His legs and his arms would become rigid; he was very stiff.

Now when he got to be around 1½ years old, my husband started saying, there's something wrong with James. Well, I didn't want to hear it. Every time I went for one of his checkups, I kept talking to his pediatrician, over and over, and he kept telling me, this kid's going to be a football player. James was never a small baby. Every time the doctor would examine him, he would fight the examination, and the doctor would say, "Boy, this kid's going to be a football player! You're going to have a lineman on your hands someday." And every time I would say to him, "He just doesn't seem to be relating to us," he'd say, "Give him time, give him time."

Our other son could read at three years old. He could go outside as a 3-year-old and tell you the constellations in the sky. And the doctor knew of Robert's intelligence, and he kept saying, "You are just comparing the two, you can't do that!" And I said, "It's not intelligence I'm talking about here, it's just how he relates to us." The doctor, on the one hand, kept suppressing my concerns; my husband, [on the other hand,] at night, would talk about it: "There's something wrong with James. I don't know what it is, but there's something wrong." And I would just say, "Well, the doctor said he's just fine, and I don't know what you're talking about." So part of me knew something wasn't right, but I would not give my husband the satisfaction [of knowing I thought] he was right. I was denying it. I was scared, I suppose, looking back on it.

One time, I was visiting my mother's house, and my sister was visiting. Now, my sister had no children. She wasn't married yet. And I remember her coming out into the kitchen, and James was in the living room. And she said to me, "You know, there's something wrong with James. You know, he's just not like Robert." And I got kind of mad. I said, "What do you mean, he's not like Robert? What's the matter with him?" [She said,] "Well there's just something about him. There's something wrong with him. He's just not with it or something." Well you know, my sister is younger than me, three years younger, and I was thinking back then, "Well. what do you know? You don't have kids, you don't know anything about them, [about] any of this." Then some more time went on, and I started to really get very concerned when he wanted to stay in his playpen all the time. He wasn't interested in exploring his world. James would still be in the playpen today if I hadn't forced him out of it.

And he never built blocks up; he always was putting them in a line. He never played with toys appropriately. If you gave him a stuffed animal, he never hugged it. I started to notice that, when I came into his room, he never stood up and waited for me with his arms up in the air to greet me, to get out of the crib in the morning, nothing. It didn't matter what time in the morning I came upstairs, he would just be sitting in the crib, in his bed, waiting for someone to take him out. And I began to realize [that] it wouldn't matter [to him] who took him out of the crib. If I left him somewhere, he never cried, never came looking for me. He didn't play appropriately, and he wasn't relating with Robert. Robert would come to me and say, "What's the matter with James, he doesn't like me," and Robert was only 4½, 5 years old.

If I took car trips with a friend, they would say, "You know, I just can't get over what a good traveler James is. No matter how long the trip is, he just sits in his little car seat, he's happy," and I'm thinking, he is too quiet. He was like in a trance. Another phrase I used to use was, he was wrapped in plastic. He was there, but there was some type of covering preventing us from being together. He was there, but I wasn't there.

He was making sounds, but he wasn't making words. So by the time he was almost 2, I was really worried. I knew something was wrong with him. We had a neighbor who was a nurse at a local hospital, and she told me about a program that came out of a local hospital. It was an early intervention program, and they would send a team of people to evaluate your child, everything from a psychologist to a speech pathologist to an occupational therapist. She had eight children, this lady next door, and she said, "You know, there's something wrong with James. I think these people should see him."

Well, I agreed, and when I went to the pediatrician, I told him about this early intervention program, and he said, "Well, you can do it if you want, but you know, I don't know if you'll find anything or not." [So] the early intervention people came and did a lot of testing and observing, numerous times, and made a report.

At the end of the report, they sat my husband and I down in our living room and told us that we really should go to Boston with him. And I said, "Well, what's the matter?" And, in some respects, they were vague. They didn't want to give me a label. They said, "Well, there's something the matter with his brain." And I said "Well, what's the matter with his brain?" And they said something like, well, he could have a tumor, he could be deaf, or there could be something else related with his brain we can't understand, and only the people in Boston could figure it out. Well, I was just sick. Now I couldn't avoid it anymore. My husband and I were both very upset.

James was a beautiful child as a young child, just beautiful. People used to remark on how beautiful he looked, all the time, and I just couldn't believe I had a child with a major problem. I just couldn't believe it. The reality had set in. So they referred us to a hospital in Boston, and we took him there. He was there for a week's evaluation, and we were not allowed to visit or see him during that week. He was about 2½ at this time.

I was upset, leaving him. I was crying. The head doctor, who was a psychiatrist and a neurologist, said to me, "What are you upset about?" And I normally don't cry, I'm not an easy person to cry. And I said, "I've never left him. He's never even been with a babysitter since he was born. I've always been with him." And this doctor said, "He's never going to be at the window looking for you. He isn't going to be calling out your name. He doesn't know who you are." And I kept saying, "But he does know who I am!" [But] the doctor was very persistent with the fact [that] no, he doesn't know who you are. I was just a person caring for him; I was no different from anybody else.

Labelling

At the end of this evaluation, which we were not allowed to go to, the doctor had my husband and I in his office, the same doctor who had said these other things to me, and he sat in his big leather chair behind his great big desk, and we were sitting in these little chairs on the other side of his office, and he said, "Well, we know what's the matter with your son now." We said, "What?" And he said, "Well it's not a brain tumor." and I was so relieved, because that whole week, you know, it's hard enough being away from him, but not knowing.

And he said, "He's not deaf, all our tests confirm that his hearing is normal." So I was happy about that, relieved, and my husband said "Well, what is it?" And the doctor said, "He's autistic." Now, I had taken psychology courses in college. I hadn't finished my degree at that time, because I dropped out to marry my husband, but my husband has a master's degree, he has two master's, actually. I had heard the word *autistic*, [but] I wasn't exactly sure what it was. It sounded familiar, [but] my husband knew exactly what the word was. And the doctor said, "Your son should really stay here in the hospital. Stay with us for a therapeutic in-house thing. You could see him Sunday afternoons. He should stay here at least a year. He needs intense therapy." And he kept saying language was the key: if he can talk, you have a chance for some type of recovery. If he can't talk, he'll never get anywhere. So he suggested to us that James come back in two weeks and stay there.

Cause

I think that autism is right up there with so many other diseases that they know nothing about, and I don't think, in my lifetime, they'll ever know. I just wish there was more money put into research, so we can find an answer to why all this happens to people like James. I see James, sometimes, dealing with his frustrations, and he's like someone trying to punch himself out of a paper bag. He's being held back by something he has no control over. I just wish they had more answers.

Maybe things have changed, if you just got a diagnosis today. I just got so frustrated going to these people, none of them being able to give us an answer. You know, if they came right out and said, well, there is no real answer, that would be one thing. But they never would say that, and that's not right. If you got a regular kid, you can go read any manual you want about how to raise a normal child, but if you have a kid who's abnormal, where do you go? Pediatricians are not much help. They're not. They end up telling you that you have the problem! Wait, give him some time, that's within the normal range, and you know it's not.

I never bought the Kanner theory, with the refrigerator mother, because I knew I wasn't like that. I knew that. As I read more about it, I realized that nobody seemed to know what caused it. All these different doctors and psychiatrists and therapists, they all had 10,000 different angles as to why children were like this, but I've come to the conclusion now that I really think it happens during conception or during the first three months of gestation. I really believe it has something to do with the chemistry of the brain, something no different than why you have dark hair and I'm wearing glasses. I really think it's something that just happens, almost like a fluke, for no reason whatsoever. It just happens.

I do think that there is a small possibility that it could be a series of things that happen within a family that eventually lead to this. Neither one of us on either side of the family had disabilities, but I do have a brother, an older brother who is extremely bright, who's a professor, who has always been considered different from other people, very eccentric at times. He's a higher mathematics kind of guy, one of the leaders in his field. I think that, perhaps, there could be a predisposition. I think all these kids are very intelligent, but I think something goes wrong with the brain wiring that does not allow them to function like other people. James had a lot of autistic savant qualities for many years, which, as he's gotten better, have diminished. Parts of his brain were unbelievable.

Grief and Sorrow

[After we were told that James was autistic,] when we got out into the hallway, I was saying to my husband (he had his back to me), "It's not that bad, he's not deaf, he doesn't have a brain tumor, we're going to get through this, it's going to be okay." And my husband was weeping, the first time I saw my husband cry since we knew each other, and he said, "Don't you understand what that doctor just told us? He's autistic. He's never going to be normal; he's always going to be disabled. He's never going to have a life, like Robert. He's never going to be like we expected him to be. It's never going to happen." And my husband was shaking me and telling me this.

And we went up and got James. When we went to find him, he didn't even remember, you know, oh, you're back to get me. Nothing. We were just the people scooping him up and taking him back home. And all the way home, we didn't even talk, we were so upset.

Day-to-Day Living

Even before he could talk, he was always fixated on numbers: numbers, numbers, numbers, numbers. If you walked from a car in the parking lot to the speech clinic, he'd say (this was when he was about 5), "Sixteen Massachusetts, 12 Connecticut." He had all the cars figured out [according to their license plates]. In the grocery store, when he was between 7 and 10, he could add up in his head everything you threw into the cart. You'd get to the register and he'd say, "$32.96, $32.96, $32.96." The cashier would go, what? It would come out exactly what he was saying. When they started doing intelligence tests, like the WISC-R, when they do the numbers sequences, he went to the highest level of being able to say things backwards and forwards. But anything having to do with comprehension, there was nothing there.

He would memorize game shows from beginning to end. And if you tape recorded it and played the show again, he had the whole thirty minutes memorized. "Hello, welcome to the Hollywood Squares! Today our guest is blah blah blah ...brought to you by blah blah blah blah." He could remember all the pitter patter back and forth, and he'd be in his room and you could hear him doing it. But yet, if you said, "Is that you talking?", he wouldn't even talk to you.

Once he started to memorize words, it didn't matter what the word was, he could spell it to you. "Industrialization: i-n-d-u-." [But] to this day, he can't tell you what some of the words he's using mean. Another thing he can do is: I'll ask, "When did we go to the cinemas last?" He'll reply, "August 23; it was a sunny day." He can tell you that.

In the past seven or eight years, he's become very into music and sports statistics, some people would say fixated. You know Billboard Magazine, that comes out on the music industry? He'd look at the whole list and, within 10 minutes, you could shut the book up, and he could tell you the name of the song, what number it is this week, what number it was last week, and how many weeks it was on the chart. He has the whole thing memorized. You could ask him [about] any year you want, he can tell you the statistics about a song. I don't care what it is. He enjoys the magazine; he gets upset if it doesn't come.

[But] he's very reluctant to discuss [these facts]; he doesn't want to tell you more. He just says, "I don't want to talk about it." Now down in Boston, that doctor I was telling you about earlier says, think of James as a human computer, the more you can get into him about life, the more he'll be able to spit out and do. And we never forgot that. James memorizes everything he does. He memorizes, [but] generalization is totally missing from his abilities.

He's a victim of routine. At one time, when he was very small, you could not even go into a grocery store, unless you went up and down the aisles in sequence, because he'd see the signs, A-B-C, 1-2-3, whatever it was, and all hell would break loose if you went down a different aisle. The doctors would say he was having a catastrophic reaction. People who wouldn't know him or know anything about me [who] saw us in the grocery store thought he was having a tremendous temper tantrum. People would come up and say, "Why don't you do something about this kid?" It would be like a panic attack. He'd get all upset: "No. No. No. Go back, go back." [He'd be] yelling and shaking and screaming and crying, and as soon as you went back into the pattern, he'd be fine.

So what I started doing [was] I would go to the store at night when nobody was there, and I would force James to go different ways, and he'd scream and yell. Of course, I'd spread it around; I wouldn't go to the same place twice, because I'd get into trouble. In fact, one guy told me not to come back the next week.

[But today James is a very different person.] He now knows how to shower and shave. He does it every night; he's very good. He's been shaving since he was 12. He wanted to grow a beard that summer and go back to school with a beard, and I said, "James, nobody who's 12 years old has a beard, I'm sorry." He went through puberty so fast.

The funniest thing he's doing, which in a way is wonderful, but in a way is aggravating, is: because he can grow a beard so fast, he always is trying to grow a mustache, grow sideburns, grow a beard no mustache, and he's got a hundred different combinations. And I'll tell him to go shave, and he comes back with a mustache, or a Fu Manchu thing. I say, "No, no, you've got to [shave it off]." [He says,] "No, I'll shave it off tomorrow." He's always experimenting. He started this last year, and he doesn't look that good with these combinations. You know, he looks much better when he shaves. He keeps telling me the other kids at school have mustaches. Of course he wants to be like the other kids, so by experimenting like this, he's noticing himself. So in a way, that's age appropriate. But yet, he's watching Sesame Street, and his whole life is splintered.

He's nearly 6 feet tall and weighs 275 pounds. Just in the past three or four months, he is slimming down. He's finally clicked about the connection about calories and gaining weight. So now I've got him looking at how many calories everything is. I figured I'd feed into his fixations. And I bought him an Easy Glider [exercise machine]. He thought [that] as soon as he got on there, he'd start shrinking, like the guy on the commercial.

'Cause he looked like the guy on the commercial before, only worse. [But] he has lost 15 pounds, and he looks trimmer. Before, if you gave him a whole bag of potato chips, he would eat the whole thing. If there's no snacks in the house, he'd eat a whole loaf of bread. He'd drink a whole gallon of milk. If the only thing in the house is Cheerios, he'd eat the entire box of Cheerios in one day.

We've had to show him how to pick up his fork, and when to put it down, and when to use a napkin, when not to use a napkin, what foods you can eat with your fingers, and what you can't, that you can't lick your plate. I mean, he'll lick a plate if you let him. And eating with your mouth closed. He'll go, "Oh, sorry, sorry." All this stuff everybody just takes for granted, he's still learning. But you can take him to McDonald's, you can take him to Burger King, you can take him to Kentucky Fried Chicken, you can take him to those places, and he'll do very nicely. A long time ago, he thought you walk in and get your food just like in the commercials, you don't have to wait. He also thought you take turns sitting with different groups. He didn't realize you had to stay with us, and I'd say, "Where are you going? No, come back!" [And he'd say,] "No, I want to eat with this family!"

My older son graduated from college out in Pennsylvania, and we wanted to go to a fancy restaurant. James could never do that. Impossible. He wouldn't have the social graces. [He would] embarrass Robert, even though Robert would probably say it's okay. The other thing was, he wouldn't want any of the food on the menu. He eats about fifteen types of food, and that's about it. He won't eat hot dogs. He likes chicken, but if you put a sauce on the chicken, he doesn't like it. [He will say loudly,] "No, no I don't like this!" So at the graduation, afterwards, we went to a place like about two steps higher than Abdow's [Big Boy Restaurant]. And they had a smorgasbord kind of thing, and he went over there to this buffet. He wanted to go and get in line, and he handled that all right. Of course, he didn't realize you could go back as many times as you want, so he comes back with all this food, six plates for himself. When he went back for dessert, he didn't like what they had. He went, "I can't eat your desserts," you know, it was real loud. But it had been a long day. And he got through the graduation very, very well. And he did find something he could eat on the smorgasbord and ate that.

At one point he would only eat five pieces of chicken. This used to be kind of a running gag behind his back, because you could get [him] five Chicken McNuggets, [and] he was just as happy as if you gave him five breasts of chicken. [If you gave him four], as long as you cut one in half, he's fine. [If you gave him six,] he wouldn't eat it. But now he'll eat 26, he'll eat 32; he'll eat any amount. But for a long time, it had to be five.

[Today] he watches a lot of television. Television is James's friend. James basically has no friends, except for us. He has one kid who's in his special ed class. He has been very kind to James. He's a higher level kid; I think [he] had anoxia at birth. He has a job at a supermarket in town, and he says, "Hi, James." They went bowling once together. But James gets no phone calls, he gets no mail.

I used to lie awake many nights, when the children were younger, and just was so upset about James having no friends.

Because I knew, as the years went by, he'd be missing out on Cub Scouts, he was missing out on this, that. I couldn't even take him to church, because the people in the baby sitting place at church didn't want him there; it was too difficult. So many things where I knew he was not having the same type of [life] as Robert was having. You see, another secret to us surviving all this was to make sure that Robert had a normal life. He was in Cub Scouts, he was in Boy Scouts, he was in extra school activities, he was on the debating team, he was on the school paper, he had his friends over. Robert basically led his life as if James was not a problem. It was like two separate worlds.

[Another problem James has] is pacing back and forth, back and forth. And usually, when he's pacing, he's talking out loud to himself. Talking about something he has to do, or something that's going to happen, or talking about Casey Cassum doing the Top 40 on the radio.

James used to go to [a teen dance hall], because they had a juke box. He loved the juke box. [He'd go by himself, because he felt he was too old to go with a parent. He would say,] "I'm 16, I'm 17," you know. I'd be a nervous wreck until he came back. Eventually, I got a call from the person managing the place, and they told me not to have James come back, because he was making people uneasy. He was loitering, because he wasn't buying enough soda, he wasn't dancing, he was just listening to the jukebox and pacing around, and they couldn't deal with it. There are just so many battles you can fight.

He's still learning phrases. If you said, "Oh, go jump off a bridge, and leave me alone," he'd look around and say, "There's no bridge around here." Many times, he talks like a foreigner. He uses the wrong tense. Not all the time, but every once in a while you catch him. If he learns a new word, he uses it continually for a month, like, "Oh, fantastic. Well, that's really fantastic. It could be fantastic if we went shopping. I want to go there for this fantastic . . ." You know, you just want to say, "Oh, give it a rest."

Also, if you really listen to him talk, he basically talks about the same things, the things he's interested in. He has a much bigger vocabulary than he had in the beginning, but in a way, it's very limited. I mean, generally speaking, he will not tolerate a long conversation. If you think of James as someone who's being interrogated at the police department, that's basically all the correspondence [you get] with him. If you had to put a developmental age on James, if you just thought of him as an 8-to-10-year-old, you'd be all set.

[The holidays were difficult] the first five or six years that we knew he had a problem. You could put a present in front of him, [and] he wouldn't even open it. He never understood what Christmas was about, or your birthday. It was just another day. You'd have to open the presents for him. You had to make a big to-do about it, show him how to use it, and that it was his present, not my present [or] your present. But now he's the first one down Christmas morning because he still believes in Santa Claus.

[He also has difficulties with feelings.] James knew my father, remembers him, but absolutely showed nothing about his death. We'd go to my mother's house, [and] of course, my father wasn't there. When I was crying and became upset about it and tried to cope with that loss, James was oblivious to the whole thing. When my mother died, he said to me, "Grandma is dead?" I said yes. He goes, okay, she's dead. He never asked me again. He never wept for her. If I died tomorrow, it would be the same thing. [He would just say,] "My mother is gone. Yes."

I laugh about this. I can see Robert holding my hand, and I'm in this semiconscious condition, and he's in this hospital room [tending to] my every whim and need, and someone says, "James, it's time to come and say good-bye to your mother," and he just puts his head in the door and says, "Bye!" I could see that happening. I don't think he has the capability of grieving.

He doesn't understand [sexual things] at all. I have never seen any evidence that he [masturbates]. I've always wondered: does he? I don't think he could unless you showed him. Of course, I would put my husband in charge of this, not me. But with my luck, I'd probably get stuck doing it. I really think that, if it became a problem, we would show him, only to relieve his sexual tensions. I had to try to explain to him how I gave birth to him, that's why I'm his mother. He just doesn't show interest.

We got a dog, thinking it would be therapeutic for James. He could care less about the dog. He thinks of the dog as a person. [He says,] "Carol, move!" He named the dog after someone on Hollywood Squares. "Move, Carol, move, you're in my way!" He doesn't want to walk the dog, he doesn't want to pet the dog, he doesn't want to feed the dog, nothing. It's just there.

As he got older, we tried to expand his world. We spent a tremendous amount of time doing that, and a big example of that is the mall. He wouldn't wait his turn. When he walked into a store, he'd walk over the threshold and shout, "Do you have a Billboard Magazine?", and they'd say, "No". [He'd shout,] "Well, you have to. Give me a Billboard Magazine." [So if he did] any of that stuff, he was out of there. So once he realized that we meant business, that we were going to pull him out of the mall, [he started learning how to behave].

We started to show him how to behave in the music store, how to wait in line, how to go to Just Fun and work the little machines in there—which he's very good at, by the way—without causing any problems, how to wait in line to get your hamburger. I would hide behind a shrub and follow him, and I'd watch him go in. To this day, I'm convinced he knew I was spying on him.

So now he goes to the mall. He has a total routine. You can sit and watch him. Well, now he's in a record store, now he's going down here, now down here. He plays the music, he plays this, he does this, he does this, he looks at this magazine in this store. He always does the same thing, and he always comes back at the same time. [But now] I don't have to spy on him.

So just a trip to the mall is a big accomplishment [when I look] back on how much we had to show him to do on his own. See, James knows he's over 18, and he'll say to you, I'm an adult. I'm not a kid, I want to be a teenager, leave me alone. But in another respect, he's saying, help me, I don't know what I am doing.

[He's has been able to stay home alone] about five years. He likes being alone. He's absolutely in heaven. He can be home alone for, maybe, five or six hours. We totally weaned him into it. [At first,] I would get in the car and just drive down the street for three or four minutes and come back. Or I had people call. Say I was out for an hour having coffee with a friend, I'd have that person call [and ask him], "Is your mother home?"

He can do any of the things you've trained him to do, if you get on his case to do it, but he won't do it on his own. He can make his own dinner, a can of Spaghetti O's or a can of ravioli. He can use the stove, he can use the microwave, if it's something you can just open up and pour in. He can cook a hamburger in the broiler oven. I usually tell him what he can have to eat, especially since he's been on this diet.

If James is home alone, I've always told him, don't answer the door, don't do this, don't do that. He'd say, "I'm here alone," he'd tell everybody. My joke is: I'll come home and find seven insurance brokers home waiting for me, with James, and them watching MTV.

Treatment

[We made our earliest decision about education after we had a diagnosis from Boston.] We decided we would convince the doctor to let us try to get help for him in Western Massachusetts, that we didn't want to keep him in the hospital. Because, you know, one minute we had our son, and within 10 minutes in a doctor's office, he's trying to take him away from us.

Well, the doctor told us we would never find people that would help us. The incidence level was too low. The people in Western Massachusetts and the hospitals were not strong enough; they didn't have the experience base that we would need. We could try if we wanted, but we would land up back there begging to have him stay there or someplace similar, that only they could provide the type of intense therapy to get him talking, possibly talking, and get him relating to some degree. James had no eye contact at that point, he was immune to pain, he showed no interpersonal relationships whatsoever, he was just there.

The only thing that would ever get him interested on any level was food. That was the only thing you could honestly say he was interested in, besides himself. And the doctor in Boston had said to us, the key to this whole thing is [to] make him more interested in your world than his. I remember that line very clearly. He also said to us that, if we would agree to come back at the end of the summer, another couple of months with James's problem wasn't going to make a bit of difference, that if it was going to make us feel better, then do it. He also emphasized again that James did not know who I was, and I'd been his primary caretaker, although, at the time, I wouldn't have known that phrase, but I know it now.

Also, you know, things have changed tremendously. When we were going through part of the [assessment] process, and my husband left to take James to the bathroom, I was asked by a social worker if James was really my husband's son, or was I harboring this secret and taking it out on James [and therefore causing James's problem]. So we went through a lot of stuff like that.

So then we went back home here, [and] we made a pact between my husband and I, and Robert to a certain extent, and as he got older definitely, that if James ever caused too much of a disruption that would start to tear our family apart, he would have to go. Because people told us we were doing the wrong thing by keeping him home: It would cause trouble for Robert, our marriage would be stressful, everything would be miserable. So we said we would take it one day at a time, but if anything got to the point where something had to give, it was going to have to be James.

I started making phone calls. I'm the kind of person that, once I know what I'm up against, I can do something about it. I can't deal in vague things, I had to have a label, I had to know what I was fighting against. So, once I had a label of autism, or childhood schizophrenia, or whatever they were going to call it (mostly those two at that time), I knew I had something to go up against. That was my enemy, as far as I was concerned. So I started making all these phone calls, begging people to help us over the summer.

What was very, very lucky, and I mean lucky, was I got in touch with Mrs. Johnson at a speech and hearing clinic. She's an unbelievable person. She was the head of the whole program, and I begged her to work with James for the summer. She said, "Bring him in and I'll look at him." Well, once she had a few minutes with James, she knew she was up against an enormous task to try and get him to talk.

He wouldn't let anybody touch him [at the clinic]. He'd

scream, he'd yell, he'd fall on the floor, he'd throw things around. He couldn't sit in a chair. He couldn't imitate speech. He had no eye contact, nothing. I told her the whole background, just like I told you. I told her about the hospital in Boston, that we had to go back there at the end of the summer. She said to me, "I will make no promises. I will take him, but you have to participate in every minute of the therapy, or I'm not going to do it." And I observed every hour. They had a two-way mirror. I was in the observation room; I watched every minute.

The first two weeks were murder. It took almost two weeks, for five hours a day, for them to get him to sit in a chair. He'd be screaming, and I'd be pacing back and forth in that observation room, wondering if I was doing the right thing. Part of me was embarrassed. People would come in to the regular clinic for speech and language therapy, and they'd hear this screaming and yelling. It was torture listening to him . They were very, very heavy on dis- cipline with him, lots of behavior modification. They would reward him with food, which probably, in retrospect, with him gaining weight, wasn't a good idea, but at the time, it worked.

We had insurance, but it was starting to run out, because they only had so much money allotted for it, and it was very expensive per hour. My parents gave me some money to help pay for it. But I mean, generally speaking, we weren't able to buy a house, because James was the house. We took no vacations, we had nothing spe- cial, nothing. It was all money poured into James, because we felt James was never going to college. This was when he needed the money. So we sacrificed anything we might want, and we've basi- cally done that all along.

So that summer, Mrs. Johnson became a god to me. She still is, to a certain degree. If she said, jump, I'd say, how high? Anything she wanted, I would do. I did total carryover into the home, and I showed my husband what he had done that day. She said, the more you can duplicate what I'm doing, the faster [he will learn]. We became really into it. Robert can tell you all his memories of end- less language therapy with James over the years.

But anyway, the three months went by like a shot, and it was the day before I had to go back to Boston for another evaluation.

Now, this evaluation was not going to be as detailed as the week's evaluation, but it was going to determine whether he should stay in the hospital or stay in Western Massachusetts with us. So the day before I was to leave, Mrs. Johnson pulled me aside to wish me luck down in Boston. Then she said something like, I've given this a lot of thought. I've done everything I can think of from my training to help James, and I think we've made some progress, because he was able to tolerate touch and he was able to sit in a chair, able to respond to certain things, able to mimic certain sounds, he seemed more with it. We have made some progress, some inroads, but I know this is an enormous task, a tremendous responsibility. And she said, "I've thought about it a lot. After you take him to Boston and have him evaluated, if they feel he should stay there, I think he should." Well, as soon as she said that, I could barely control myself. I got out into the parking lot, and I cried all the way [home], just like I had all the way from Boston, because I felt just like my whole world was falling in all over again. I was going to have to sacrifice him being with us in order to get him the help he needed, and I'd never be able to do anything for him. They were going to do everything, and I was just starting to feel close to James. Not that you could, but compared to what it was 6 months before, I felt like I was. And even my mother was starting to notice he seemed a little bit different, and other people were commenting: he's changing.

So I went down to Boston again, with my husband and Robert and James, and they evaluated him again, and the doctor said. "Well, you have made some progress; there is a definite change. But you're never going to be able to put together [what he needs] up in Western Massachusetts. There aren't enough trained people. They don't know what we know. I really think you should leave him here. So," he said, "why don't you go home, get his things, and come back in a week or so, and we'll admit him."

My husband and I went home, and we fought about it all over again, and we said, if we could find Mrs. Johnson, maybe we could find other people. We'd given this a lot of thought, and talked to the school department, because at this point, before you know it, he was going to be three, and the school was willing to pay for anybody to help us instead of paying the bills down in Boston. The reality of it was something like $25,000 a year for him to stay down there. I think now it would be, like, $40,000 a year.

We asked the doctor if he could help us up here, and he said, "I'll only do it if you come here every three months. We'll set up a program where you have to come down here, so I can track his progress, give him tests, and see how he is doing, and guide you with the people up there." And we said yes, we'd be more than willing to do that, but we were just not willing to give him up. We just could not give our son away. We couldn't do it. So we stayed up here, and with the help of the public schools and a lot of other people, including Mrs. Johnson, we started all these other programs. The school department paid me to drive him to therapy programs, so we drove 249 miles a week, back and forth, and I observed all the time, and we got him an aide. He was into so many programs. Everything had to be created, because James was the only kid with this problem, so that's what we did. And we kept going down to Boston, and then he started to talk. And that was after hundreds and hundreds of hours of language therapy. When James first started talking, I remember Robert coming to me and saying, "I finally have a brother. He's talking to me."

[Today James is in a special education program at our local high school, and we are looking into a vocational placement.]

[James does have some awareness that he has a disability.] When he was about nine or ten years old—I always remember this as a big turning point—he went up to bed, and I said good night to him, and I came back downstairs. My husband was working. And all of a sudden, out of nowhere, James was at the top of the stairs, and he was weeping. And he never cries, never. And I thought, something had happened to him. He was up at the top of the stairs, and I said, "What's the matter, what's the matter?" He said, "I want to start over. I want to be a baby again. I want to be like Robert. I don't like being me." I think it finally clicked inside his head, and he said, "I can't talk good. I can't do a lot of things." He was talking about his limitations in his own way. And I reassured him, I took him back to bed, said that we were always going to be there to help him. And yeah, he did have trouble talking, that was true, and he did have trouble thinking, that was true, that he was right. But that didn't mean that he couldn't get better.

[For] the past year and a half, he's been medicated. He never took medication in his whole life [before that]. We fought, because we didn't want to shroud him. When he was a child and in a day program, they wanted to medicate him with Haldol. They felt that, behaviorally, it would calm him down, and we could reach him more, and we said, you know, he's talking more, we want the real James, we don't want someone medicated, so he'll sit better in class. We want to get the most information into him. So we fought them there. And when we were in Boston once, I asked the doctor, "Should we medicate him or not? I'm getting a lot of pressure from the school to do it," and the doctor said, "Only do it if you need a break, because that's why they want to do it."

Since he has been on the medication, he has paced less. And it has made a difference in his sociability. I'm not saying he's the life of the party, and I'm not saying he could have a conversation like we're having, [but] he's willing to offer information. Like, he might come in the room and say, "Did you see that show on CNN?" He never would have said that prior to the medication.

Stresses on the Family

Many of the couples we knew from support groups over these years had tremendous marital problems. Many of them are divorced, but especially when it was the sons who had the problems. The husband couldn't cope. In particular, that combination seemed to be the worst. [But] Kevin has stood by James through thick and thin. He really has. Never been ashamed of James, always been there. And like I said, he was the first person to notice James wasn't right. He's always been there for him.

Kevin and I have had our bad times. We were separated for a couple of months after my father died and Kevin lost his job. I was working two jobs and dealing with the kids, and Kevin was working the night shift as an EMT. You know, we've had our low points. I won't pretend we haven't. But compared to other families, once we got through the first five years with James' problem, we've done quite well.

I think the negative side of Robert's life with James, if there is one, is that, as he goes into his adulthood, if he marries, if he has children, there's a big question mark as to what's going to happen to his kids.

After I had James, I stopped having children on purpose, because I couldn't deal with this in another child. I just felt James had been victimized, and I wasn't going to do that to somebody else. You know, I just couldn't put another child through that kind of a life. And the doctor said to me, "Well, you had Robert, he's fine. You could have another child who's perfectly okay." I said, "But I had James. Look at all the problems he's got." I was traumatized about it.

[Robert has] never dated. I think that's part of the thing that holds him back. I mean, he likes girls, he likes being around them. He's very comfortable with them, but he puts his education first. He's very serious about getting his doctorate now, and that's all that matters.

If you talked to Robert, you would think he was 33, but he's not. When he was young, I wanted to shake him and say, "Act like a 9-year-old, please," because he was so much like an adult. I do think the whole James situation impacted him, and he was much more aware and mature, and he had more worries going to school than the average kid sitting next to him in his classes. And you know, he also had no other siblings. So it was just us and James, and I don't think that helped.

I was glad he went to [college,] because it got him away from here. He needed to get away. He didn't say that, but it gave him total freedom. He wouldn't have to explain to people about James.

Coming back this year has been kind of a rude awakening. He hasn't been home with us for four years, except for the summer. And James is a totally different person now; we're all adults. I think it's good for Robert. He sees the hours I work. You know, he's got a better feel for what the family is all about.

But we're encouraging him to apply to schools no matter where they are. So I think, once he leaves again, he'll come more into his own and start dating.

The ripples of this go on forever. That's something people

don't understand if they don't live with this. It's not just James's problem, it's everybody's problem, and it echoes out all over the place in different ways.

I don't think I would have become a special education teacher if I didn't have to deal with James. [I stopped teaching because] I got burned out. See, I'm the type of person who always wants the best of everything. And when I had a chance, once James got into a full-day program where I didn't have to be responsible for him and I didn't have to watch his therapies anymore, I went back to school. And I took 20 to 22 credits a semester, and I finished in two years. I graduated second out of my class.

I wanted to work with autistic kids. I wanted to work with parents who were in the same predicament as I had been in, [but] I had to get a job around here, because of my family. I couldn't just leave, so I winded up substituting, and I worked with juvenile delinquents for 2½ years.

I was assaulted four times. I collected knives before school started. Kids were wearing their street colors. Verbal abuse, threatening, you name it, I listened to it for 2½ years. Well, I did that plus took care of James. Then I stopped doing that, and I got my first job working with autistic kids. I did that for a year. It was at that point that Kevin and I separated for two months. I was also doing respite care [during the] summers, for other people, for adult retarded people, so their families could have a break.

What I didn't anticipate, when I went off into the world of special education, was that I needed a break. I didn't think. James had become such a way of life to me. I didn't realize that I was having all this stress during the day, whether it's working with juvenile delinquents or autistic young kids, and then coming home to James, and summers I had the other people plus James. I never had a break.

I feel now, looking back on my whole experience, going to get my special education degree was probably the best thing I ever did, because, when I go to those team meetings, I know how to write an ed plan, I know if they're giving me a song and dance, I know how the school systems do their strategies. It helped me a lot to program for James. I never had to have someone explain terms to me.

Kevin and I, since Robert became a senior in high school, have gone away a couple of nights a year, alone. We've never taken a vacation together, with James, never, never, you know, and I feel cheated on that sometimes, that we just can't be like somebody else. We did when we went to Robert's graduation, [and] a couple of times we went to New York. But he had to be in the same room with us, because he couldn't be alone.

Long Range Forecast

Our game plan right now is to keep him in school with a vocational base, to do a half-day placement, then get him into working a job [while] still living at home, then get him into a group home. I'm still relatively young, you know, more or less. I don't want James with me when I'm 60 years old. As soon as James is ready to live in supervised housing, I'd be all for it. Our goal is to, eventually, have him go into group living, but only after going to work every day and getting comfortable with the routine. Then we're going to wean him out of the house.

By the time I am, like, in my fifties, I would like to see James coming over to see me at night for dinner, coming weekends and spending the weekends, and living somewhere else, supervised, within the town.

Even though you are his parents, you have to [obtain guardianship of him once he turns 18. It] took us a year to do it, a year and a half, actually. If you don't go for guardianship and something happens [that brings your child into court], when they reach 18 or over, the courts are [not necessarily] going to make you the guardian. Just because you've been his primary caretakers and his parents doesn't mean anything, because the first thing the court's going to say is, why didn't you go for guardianship, if you knew this might happen? And that's the main reason you have to go before they're 18.

My husband and I do not want James to go into the Department of Retardation, or whatever, without us being the decision-makers. I don't want decisions being made on his behalf. I have seen too many people lose control of their adult children because of that. You see the homeless; they can't make their own decisions.

When all this happened to us with James, the biggest thing I had to do was accept James for who he was, when he was very young, because I didn't expect James to be this way. And I really had to mourn the loss of the child I never got. All the dreams that I thought about, just when you're pregnant and thinking about your children, all went down the drain, and that child did not exist. That child was never going to be there, and we had to settle for what we had left, what was given to us, and at first, that was very difficult. Once I accepted James for who he was and not who I thought he was supposed to be, it got better, because I knew what I was up against, and I was not going to let this whole situation defeat us. I was so determined that James was going to get better.

We kept trying and trying and trying and trying, and they said he'd never ride a bike. Well, he rode a bike. At first, he never stopped at stop lights or at curbs, and he just went whipping across intersections. But, eventually [he learned how to do it safely].

But then you get into this false sense of everyday living, where James is James, and everything isn't that bad, and he's different from my friends' sons, but that's okay. And then all of a sudden, BOOM, guardianship time, and, BOOM, what do we do? And everybody's telling us to put him on Social Security, because he's developmentally disabled, and it all comes home to roost again. You can look back and pat yourself on the back and say, "You know, we've done a darn good job, we never bailed out on him. We've been there step by step. He's got a life now. He's confused at times, but he's got a life." But then, the other side of that is [that] you have to face the realities all over again, that he isn't like everybody else.

He has tremendous shortcomings, even with the progress that he's made, and the whole guardianship procedure just validates that, and so does the going for Social Security. So it's like another slap in the face, even though you know you're doing the right thing. Just like breaking open a wound, but the only reassurance you have is you know you have to do it. Part of me kept saying, maybe I'll never have to. But then, when I was sitting in the courtroom and the lawyers were discussing his case—they were very good about not using certain terms in front of him, because I asked them not to—it was upsetting.

The medication became an issue, all sorts of lawyers investigating whether we were misusing the drugs on him. It wasn't just smooth sailing. but it all worked out fine. In fact, one of the women (James had two lawyers appointed by the court on his behalf) said, "I want you to come see me at my office, James." I sent flowers to her, from James, to thank her.

If I say to James, "What do you want to do for a job?", for a long time [he would say] he wanted to put billboards up, because he liked the cigarette billboards with the numbers, low in tar and nicotine, in the corner.

When we went down to Pennsylvania to Robert's school—there's 396 billboards between here and Pennsylvania, in case you're wondering. [He counted] everyone. One, two, he goes; he's driving me crazy. And then, when we get down there, it says, "Welcome to [the college]," He says, "Keep going, I need four hundred!" And I said, "Forget it!" And he's yelling at me and on Robert's campus, which is so serene—it used to be an arboretum, you know, and it's so quiet, with these little swans over here, and our van is rocking back and forth, and James is yelling at me, "Go BACK! We need four more billboards!" It was bad.

Then, from there, he didn't want to put billboards up, he wanted to go to Pittsburgh and become a Pittsburgh Steeler. And I said, "James, you are not in regular high school. You cannot just go to Pennsylvania and become a Pittsburgh Steeler." Now, if I didn't have the guardianship, he could get up tomorrow morning and say I'm going to Pittsburgh!

He's learning to take the bus now. But what if he got into a verbal argument with the bus driver, because he hadn't flipped the sign yet? The guy pushes him off the bus, and James pushes him back, and the guy hits his head. James goes to court for assault. With the guardianship, they look at James totally different. Now, I'm not saying he'd get off the hook, but it's safe to assume they'd take into consideration Social Security and guardianship.

We have a backup guardian to take our places, one by one. [We've got Robert] and my youngest brother, who is only 10 years older than Robert. By then, James will be in supervised housing, so it will be more like they don't have to be with him, [just look over his affairs financially, and whatever]. That's the game plan.

To me, the whole idea of being a parent to any child is to parent them so they can get along in the world without you, because
someday you're not going to be there, and, no matter when that is,
you want them to be healthy, happy, functioning, capable of doing
their own daily living jobs, making decisions without you. If you
do your job, they don't need you. That's a compliment, if you've
done your job. It's no different with James. So the negative thing is
[that] you have to be much more aware, when you have a disabled
child, about getting him ready to not have you there. Like the
guardianship, and the housing: there's a tremendous amount of
work. You constantly are worried about what's going to happen to
him when you're not there any more. I had a friend, who I have not
talked to in a long time. Her son is autistic, severely disabled, and
she told me, point blank, that when the time came, she would take
her life and his, because she would not leave him behind.

Social Stigma

The harassment that he [has] received [over the years is] unbelievable! I became a real bum to the school; I was always complaining.
It got to the point where I had to go to people's homes and tell
them I would press charges. I'll just name off some things that happened to him: from the time he was 10 or 11 until he was 17, rocks
were thrown at him, hitting his head; he was spit on; he was beaten
up, more than once; he was beat up in the bathroom; he was beat
up in the locker room, kids all over him, putting things in his hair;
he was yelled at constantly, names like, hey, retard, stupid, tremendous amounts of obscenities. They were making remarks about
oral sex to him, things he didn't even understand. He would be
home, and people would be going by the door of our house, yelling
at James inside, taunting him. They would call him up on the telephone and yell at him on the phone. We had to have our number
changed.

The teachers kept saying, "We do the best we can. These kids
know how to push all his buttons." And as soon as James got very
upset, he was the one sent home, 'cause he was out of control, and
he was handicapped, and he was disturbed, so he should go home.

I went to the principal when he was in the junior high school, and I said, "James is being crucified on a daily basis at your school." [He replied,] "Well, we all get crucified in our job, and as an adult, I do too, and he just has to learn to take it." James isn't doing anything. He's just the butt of all this.

[One day,] I got a call from this lady down the street, and she told me that she saw kids doing terrible things to James on his bicycle, terrible: pushing him down, beating him up, spitting on him, kicking him, punching him. Eventually, I found out the name of one of these kids, so I spent the whole weekend going to homes in that area of town. I'd knock on the door and I'd say, "My son, James, is a special ed student in your school, and we live on Main Street, and I have reason to believe your son has been harassing my son, because somebody has seen it, and he is one of many kids who have been doing this, and I mean to put a stop to it. I need to talk to you." Well, this is so out of character for me, you wouldn't believe it.

All but two of the parents agreed that their sons were capable of doing the same kind of thing. And I said that, if I saw anything else happen, or if I had a person that I knew, like this woman down the street—if she witnessed it again, she would be willing to testify. I will take you to court for assault, because, I said, my son is being traumatized by these kids, just because he's different. And I am so sick of hearing all these years, "Oh, kids are kids, and kids can be mean." But there's a level to everything, and to me, these kids had gone over the line. And that was the last I ever saw of those kids bothering James.

Prior to this—I've got to tell you this story, because it shows you how far I got pushed—James and I went over [to a mall, food shopping,] on a Saturday. We see these kids on their bikes on their way to the mall, and I said to James, "Those kids look about your age." We get into Ames [Department Store], and James and I used to split up, and he'd go over and look at the calculators and the digital stuff and the TVs and the record players and tape players and music stuff, and I'd go do my shopping, and we'd meet.

I had not been away from him for five minutes when I heard him screaming and yelling and carrying on and saying, "Help me. Help me. Help me." I go running over to this clothing area where he is, and there were four kids, three boys and a girl, punching him, kicking him, calling him names, right in Ames, right in the clothing section, laughing at him.

When they saw me coming, they figured out I must be with him, and they all hid behind the clothing racks, and they were laughing. Then they started calling me names, that I was the retard's mother and stuff like this. James was 13 or 14 at the time.

So what I did was, I told James to leave the store right away, and he was going to go to the bookstore that was right near Abdows [Big Boy Restaurant], then I would meet him at the Food Store in 15 minutes.

And I stood—I knew these were the same kids I saw going over there; I saw their bikes were outside—so I went, and I stood at the exit to the store, right next to their bikes. I wanted to slash their tires, that's what I really wanted to do, 'cause they had James all worked up, and he had told me they were some of the kids bothering him.

I stood outside and I waited, and they're peering through the windows looking at me, and going back and talking to each other; I could see them. And finally, the girl comes out and just pretends that she's not with them. She comes over to me, and I said, "You come out to check out how you're going to get your bikes back?" She says, "Well, I'm not with them." I said, "Listen, you go back. You're a bunch of cowards. You get your kicks picking on someone who's disabled? You're not doing this anymore. Go back and tell your friends that they're not getting their bikes back until they talk to me."

So she goes back, and they're all talking. Well, I was beginning to realize that James is going to be waiting for me, and I have to leave, [so I left]. As soon as I got to my car, they come scurrying out, and they drove further away from me and looked like they were going to drive in front of me, but instead of pulling out to go towards the food store there, they rammed my car, yelling obscenities at me. This is how violent these kids are.Then, after they rammed my car, they went in front of me, way in front of me, and stood and were doing obscene gestures at me, saying, "Come on, hit us, come on, hit us," the four of them.

Honest to God, I lost it. I put my foot down on the accelerator and went right after them, like a bowling ball heading towards the pins. And I snapped out of it right before I hit them. I almost hit all four of them. I just missed them. I was so angry, because, to me, those kids represented all the kids who had been bothering him, harassing him, and doing these things to him.

It was the first time I had seen these kids face to face, and oh, I was so upset. Then I got control of myself, and said, what am I doing? I could have hurt those kids. Thank God I didn't, but I came really close. I was so angry. The day was so upsetting to me; the whole afternoon was a nightmare. I said to myself, James puts up with this day after day after day for years? It's against the law to do this or that with other people who are different, but anybody can say anything to someone who's disabled and get away with it. The disabled are everybody's doormat.

Surviving and Transcending

James has enriched our lives. I think I'm a better person because of James. I don't take things for granted. I appreciate other people's problems more than I would have. If they have a child who isn't like everybody else's, I'm much more sensitive.

I could never have given anybody any advice when I first started out on this road. I mean, I was impossible, [but] now that I've been dealing with this since he was 2½ ([and he's] now almost twenty), the first thing is I would say to a parent for advice is to accept him for who he is. That was a big difference to me. You have to learn not to feel guilty. Seeing him do everything he has done has been ten times more rewarding than if he had been a normal child. But if you had told me that in the beginning, I wouldn't have believed you. So you have to give yourself some time.

The other thing is [that] you have to be willing to go out and find people that will help you and tell you you're an important person on the team of helping. And you have to be willing to get involved. You can't stay on the outside; you have to be part of the change. Don't be unrealistic, but don't give up. My mother used to say, "Tomorrow could be better than today." If you think everything's going to be miserable, it's going to be miserable. You have to find humor. We've had a lot of funny things with James. We've had to learn to laugh at things.

I've got to tell you a funny story. In the summer, James swims and lifts weights at [a local] college with my husband. He is a very good swimmer; he swims like a baby porpoise. He swims laps, back and forth and back and forth. He does 32 laps and comes home. Not 31, not 33. When James would be doing his repetitions, my husband would be weightlifting. From there, they'd take a shower. Well, James has never taken communal showers with other men, so Kevin got him to do this. So this is funny. They're both in there taking showers. Kevin's like way at that end of the shower area, James is over here, and Kevin's got his hair all soaped up, and he's lathering up. There's all these other men scattered through the shower place, [and] James yells, "Dad!" And Kevin goes, "What, James?" [James yells,] "I haven't seen you naked in a long time!" [Kevin was] so embarrassed!

The other thing [you need to do], which I haven't done, is give yourself a break. My husband and I have been on such a treadmill for so long, we don't know what it's like not to be. You know, always on our guard. You need to have more of a support system than what we've had.

One thing that I did was [that] I always talked to people who were ahead of me. When James was two, I talked to people who had 7-year-old kids who had problems. When he was seven, I was talking to people who had kids who were 12. When he was 12, I was talking to people whose kids were 18. I would have never known what steps to take next if I hadn't done that.

And the other thing is, I think, you really have to be a close family. If you're a selfish family, you'll never give enough of yourself to help a child with these kinds of problems. Some people that I've met along the way were unable to take care of their children. They knew they couldn't do it, so they let other people do it. And it wasn't because they didn't love their child, it was because they knew they couldn't handle it. And people put them down for that, which was wrong. But they knew what their limitations were.

I have discovered a tremendous amount of things about myself through this journey. You know, I'm a lot stronger than I ever thought I was. I have a lot more endurance. You know, people that know me think I'm really a wonderful person, but I'm no saint. But I've discovered things about myself. I'm a better parent than I would have been if my kids had both been normal, I know I am.

The worst thing you can do is feel isolated. But when James first started [having problems], I thought I was the only person in the world that was up against any of this. I'd say to people [who asked] what's the matter with James, "He's autistic." "He draws?", they'd ask. "No, no. He doesn't draw."

But I've become a stronger person, I've learned to, I really have. I think he's opened up doors for me, and I think I've contributed to other people's lives because of James, which, otherwise, I probably never would have done. You know, I would never have had a vested interest in other people's children, or their problems, if he hadn't been around.

I tell the young people that work in here with me for the summer: "Someday, when you think about me, and you say, 'What did I learn from her?,' what you've learned from me is this: You take in life what's given to you, and you make the best of it. You are going to have a lot of problems in life you do not have control over, but you can get control over them. And once you feel you are in control, you can turn the situation around and make the best of it. But it's a lot of work, and you've got to be willing to do it." That's what I've done, basically.

Chapter 7
The Pilot

 Randy is 22-years-old and lives with his adoptive mother, Tammy. He was adopted when he was 17 days old. At one time, he also lived with his adoptive father, who died when Randy was seven years old, and his adoptive sister, Mariann, who is now married and living on her own. The interview was with Tammy, who works in the office of a local company. She met me after work in my office. The day before the interview, Randy had broken his ankle. Tammy brought pictures to show me how handsome Randy is.

Diagnosis

I have to be honest and say [that] the first 24 hours that I had him, I knew there was something wrong with him. [He was] too quiet, too good. There were many times I had gone to check in on the crib and I thought he was dead, because he was so still.

He had such bed sores [that I brought him] to the doctor for treatment of them, after a day or two. And I remember mentioning how quiet he was. He was just eerie. I was told he was checked out, and he was fine. He just had bedsores. It just continued until I made such a nuisance of myself, and then I was put on a guilt trip, and I was told, was I looking for something wrong with him, because he wasn't my natural child? and I should be happy that I had such a good child.

I think my husband [thought something was wrong, too,] but he didn't want to believe it. It was easier for him not to acknowledge it. My mother thought there was something wrong. He threw up on her every time she touched him. He was always stiff, except with me. He always allowed me to touch him. He would allow my husband, too, but he was still stiff about it, and with me, he was a little less stiff.

[Finally,] I just walked into a mental health clinic. I called them up crying, "Something is wrong with my baby." I had brought him to a little daycare type thing, and they had told me to bring him home. He wouldn't associate with the other children. All he would do is go off by himself. He would flutter, twiddle his fingers, and flap his arms and make little cluck noises. [At the mental health clinic,] they interviewed us first and then took him [to see] a psychologist or psychiatrist. I remember them bringing him back into the room to me and saying, "Your baby is very sick."

I was frightened when they told us. I knew it, and I wanted to know, but when I was told, I was scared. I didn't know what was wrong with my baby, and I didn't know how to help him, and it didn't have a name. We couldn't even look it up. It was really hard.

Labelling

This was in an era when it was almost against the law to label children. You couldn't say they were retarded or [had] Down syndrome. They were special needs, and that's what they said: he was special needs.

Now that we look back on his behaviors and mannerisms, now [that] it has a name, it was definitely autism. I think there are 12 or 13 characteristics of autistic people. He just displayed all 12 or 13 at one time, but they couldn't give it a name, because we were in that era when it was pretty much against the law to label a child.

[We were first told Randy had autism] when he was around nine or ten years old, [when] I had taken him to be monitored in Worcester. [He had a CAT scan,] and it showed he had damage to the temporal lobe area. I tried to find material on autism [after that,] and there was very, very little material I could get my hands on. It was still the unknown illness.

Cause

When he was presented to us [at the orphanage], we were told it was a normal delivery with absolutely no complications. [We were given only some] very, very general information about his birth and nationality and some of his mother's interests, and that's about it. It wasn't until Randy was about nine or ten years old—I was bringing him to a new doctor in Worcester and had gotten all the medical records and a birth record on him and was going through everything—that I saw the birth record, which was completely different from what I had been told. We were told everything was normal, but a breech birth is not normal, nor is 18 hours of labor.

Day-to-Day Living

Randy's whole life [today] is a ritual. It has [to be,] so he can function comfortably. He goes to bed at 10 o'clock. He has an order in
which he does things: pajamas, medicine, water, bathroom, bed.
He still doesn't turn the light off. He thinks that, when you don't
have a light on, lights come at him in the dark and frighten him.

He has an alarm. He sets it himself and gets up himself. He
dresses himself and makes his own breakfast. He [even] irons his
own clothes, [which] got to be cool, whatever cool is. I usually go
to the mall and look at what I think the cool guys are wearing, and
then I bring it home. He won't shop; I shop for him. He finds shopping very stressful. It's even down to his sneakers. They could be
too small, but he'll say they're fine.

[He has issues around privacy] with everyone. In fact, when I
take him to the doctor, or if I say, "Randy, we have to go to the
doctor," he'll say, "They're not going to make me take my clothes
off." He has a thing about not wanting to take his clothes off. He
gets very, very nervous and loud about it.

He'll eat just about anything, [but] he would prefer to eat
spaghetti and sauce. For him, it's [spaghetti and sauce] 365 days a
year, and that's okay, [if] I let him. I make sure the sauce has meat
in it, and he loves it. There's a batch of sauce made every Saturday,
and I make lasagna too. He likes anything in the lasagna and
spaghetti family. At school, he eats in the cafeteria, and I think he
basically eats almost the same thing every day.

He doesn't like leftovers. Spaghetti [or other soft foods], he'll
eat leftover, but if I was to make a meat loaf, if that's what he
wanted, and there was meat loaf left over, he won't touch it. It
makes him gag. There's just something about it [having been] left
over in the refrigerator.

He only eats one item at a time on his plate; otherwise, he
won't eat. If we have a roast, potatoes, gravy, vegetables, whatever,
he'll eat all of one thing before he moves to the other thing. And he
always has his drink very last, and he gulps. He opens his throat
and it goes down on him. He has a little difficulty cutting. He can
do it, [but] if he's struggling for a real long time, I'll ask him if he
wants me to cut it for him, and he'll say yes. But I always let him

struggle himself for a while. Another thing that he does, which I think is kind of odd, and he's always done it, is [that] he pulls the chair all the way up to the table, until the table is actually touching his body.

He doesn't seem to have a desire to be out in the neighborhood where the kids are. I guess that is uncomfortable for him. He [does have] grownup friends in the neighborhood that he visits. He's ridden his bike and made friends with people on another street, who have no children, and once in a while, he'll call them and ask if he can visit. They're very good to him. They think Randy's great. And even, once in a while, they'll call and say they're going out for soft serve [ice cream] and could they take Randy with them. I don't even know the people. These are friends of Randy's that he just made on his own. I've spoken to them, and they are very aware of Randy's autism, and they're very comfortable with it.

Getting him to be involved [used to be] a problem. He would always be off by himself, to the side, just quiet. [But now] he has many, many, many friends at church. We belong to an Assembly of God church, and he is very, very accepted by the church, by the youth [group] and by the singles. He's kind of, like, in with the singles, and he's in with the youth as well, because he can get along with both groups.

He goes out with the singles after Wednesday night service. They go to McDonald's or Friendly's or whatever, and he's part of that group, and they're very good to him, and he also goes out Sunday night. He gets his own ride home, and he's got some good friends there. And the church is very active, too, so he goes to whatever activities the youth or the singles are having. He's always part of it.

They just had a thing at [the amusement park]. Once a month, they rent out the roller rink [there], just a Christian night. He goes to that. He watches some TV, he likes videos, and he likes cassette tapes. He looks at magazines and books. He likes Star Trek, and he's been kind of interested in cartoons.

He goes to Christian [camp] for a week every July, which the church [sponsors], and he stays overnight for the whole week. He's in a cabin with four other fellows, and there's, of course, a counselor in each cabin. And he does really well. The man that directs it is also a special education teacher. He's known Randy for years and years, and they keep a close eye on him.

This Saturday, if the weather holds, he's going to go flying. One of the fellows in church is a pilot, and Randy put his share in for the gas, and up they're going to go. He loves flying; he just thinks flying is wonderful. That's sort of his fixation: memorizing volumes of information about airplanes. He can tell you the weight of every aircraft, with or without fuel, and the wingspan. Everything and anything you could possibly want to know about them, any type of airplane: he's memorized this, and it's important to him. He's always wanted to be a pilot, and if you ask him what he wants to do, he'll tell you he wants to be a pilot. But now he also will tell you, "I have some brain damage, and I'm autistic, and I don't think I can do that." He's not happy about it, but just recently, within the last two years, he is really beginning to accept some of his limitations. As soon as I knew [he had autism, he was told, but] just recently he realized what it meant. And he's angry about it. It's not like he's saying this nicely, "But I can't." You would see that this is really frustrating and hard for him, [that's he's thinking,] Why do I have to be like this?

Other people his age have girlfriends and drive a car and date and go to lounges and drink beer and watch football games and play football and that kind of thing, and Randy doesn't do that. He doesn't drive, [and] he doesn't have a girlfriend, [although] he'd love one. He talks about it: "I wish I could get a girlfriend. I wish I could get a girlfriend." He wants to get married and have a child. I'm going to talk to him about sterilization one of these days.

I took him to [a] hospital for a disabled driver evaluation test. And he went through the whole test, psychological, actual steering wheel and brake, and things coming at you, and whatever, and he failed. I knew he would. I was praying that by some slim chance he wouldn't make it through this thing.

He didn't do well, and they didn't feel that he should drive a car, and he did sign a waiver that was sent to the registry of motor vehicles, saying that he was signing off on it. Once he said to me, "You made me sign that paper," and I said, "No, Randy, you know

I didn't make you. We explained it to you, and we advised you. We thought this was the best thing for you to do, but I did not make you sign it." And he agreed. But you know, he was trying to put the blame on me. I think if he would take the test today, he would pass it. He memorized everything, because they told him the answers.

This was about two years ago, so he would have been about 20. Psychologically, he had a real difficult time with that. He cried when he found out he would never be able to drive a car, so I spoke to the mental health clinic. We had dealt with them on and off. He's been going for two years now, every Tuesday.

Last week, when I was picking him up from skating, and we were driving to McDonald's, I said, "Randy," (because there was a girl murdered in our town recently,) "If people stop and ask you directions, I don't want you talking to anybody, just keep walking." [He said,] "I can't do that, Mom, they'll get mad at me. Already people have asked me how to get someplace, and I know, so I tell them." I said, "Randy, I don't feel good about this. We've got a crazy person out there, what's to say they're not going to pull you in the car?" [He said,] "What am I going to do? They're going to think I'm stupid." I said, "No, just keep walking, just ignore them."

I guess he thought about it, because about a week passed, and we were driving from McDonald's to the roller rink, and he said, "What should I do if a car stopped, and the man wants directions, and he's got a gun, and he says to me, 'Get in the car and drive.'?" I said, "Then you need to tell him that you have brain damage and that you can't drive." [He said,] "Well, don't you think the man is going to get mad?" And I said, "Randy, if he's stopping and he's got a gun, he's probably mad already. You just need to keep saying to him, 'I have brain damage and I can't drive.' Okay?" And he said, "Okay, Mom, then that's what I'll do."

[He] still has a problem with [safety. He has] like tunnel vision. We're here and the car is there. [He says,] "I'm going to the car," [and steps right out into traffic.] And he gives me a heart attack! They've worked on that in school, until he was giving them a heart attack too. I try to stay ahead of it. We'll come out of church, and we're getting near the sidewalk, and I'll say, "You know you got to watch for cars, right? Okay, because you don't want to give me a heart attack." [And he'll say,] "Oh, I know, I know." [But] sometimes still, he'll just step out without thinking.

[Another thing he does is] he mimics. He can be anybody, any sound, any creature; he's perfect. Makes me crazy! [For example,] we just took a trip for Easter, to visit my friends. He decided he liked [my friend,] Mr. Smith's, voice, so for the whole 6 days we were there, he's Mr. Smith. It made me crazy. He would talk like him, so anything Randy spoke about, he spoke just like Mr. Smith. I just screamed, "You're making me crazy," and he just [said,] "But I like Mr. Smith's voice." I told him: "I know, I do too, and I love Mr. Smith, but I don't want to hear Mr. Smith coming out of you, because it's making me crazy." [He does] animal voices [too]. I have to ask him if it's him or the dog, because I can't tell. [I'll ask him,] "Did the dog make the noise, Randy, or was that you making the noise?"

He [also] talks to himself, and he answers himself, and it makes me nuts! Most of the time, it's soft enough where I'm not sure if he was talking to me or not, and then I'll ask him, "Are you talking to me, Randy? Are you saying something important here? Should I be listening to you or what?" And then he won't answer me, because he knows [that] if he does, he'll [have to] tell me he's just talking to himself, [and] I'm going to get mad.

We worked out, with a psychologist, kind of an understanding about this. I'm understanding more that Randy needs to do this, that it makes him feel good inside. It actually gives him a physical [sense] of well-being. He does this out of necessity, so we've agreed that, if he really needs to do this, then he has to do it in his room with his door shut, so it doesn't make me crazy. [He also needs to control this behavior because] it's inappropriate. It makes him look strange; it makes people look at him strangely. He doesn't want to be different, and he's beginning to think that, when he does this out in public, he's drawing attention to the fact that he is different.

He has big trouble with eye contact. It's very, very difficult for him to keep eye contact. I work on that with him. He'll [let his eyes] come in [contact with yours] for a minute, and then it's very uncomfortable for him. He'll have his head down often times. We're working on the fact that [this is a problem. I say to him,] "It's hard to understand you, Randy, you know, when the waitress wants your order, it's hard for her to understand you when your chin is down. I understand it's hard for you, but look at her."

I'm always talking to him, always, always, always. I try to do it in a way that I'm not coming down on him. I try to set it up ahead of time in a very laid back manner, so that I'm not preaching to him or at him. I'm trying not to nitpick at everything he's doing. I try to work it in a way that he's not intimidated by it.

He [can] read at the fourth grade level, maybe fifth grade, and he has difficulty signing his name. I am his legal guardian, so I can sign for him. When we were in the emergency room for his fractured ankle, there were papers to be signed, and the lines are small, and Randy writes very large. He has a hard time fitting his signature on the little line. He writes in cursive with a lot of stops. He does it slow. Going from printing to cursive was very difficult for him, and he doesn't like to write. He doesn't like the way his writing is, and he grumbles about it. [He'll say,] "Would you write this for me, Mom?" [If I reply,] "Why don't you write it Randy?", [he'll say,] "I don't like my writing, it's like a baby." I say, "Randy, I think your writing's great. I can understand it." I always give him the option. [I'll say,] "Randy, they need you to sign on this line, from here to here. Do you want to sign, or do you want me to?" And sometimes he says, "Okay," and he signs it, and other times he says, "No, Mom."

One of the hardest things with Randy is language and his language perceptions, even, like, with his [broken] ankle. I said to him, "Is it throbbing?" He didn't know what it meant. He could relate to an ache, but not a throb. And when I sat down and thought about it, I thought, well, what really is the difference between something aching and something throbbing. Now somehow in my mind, there's a difference. I can think about it. And I sat with him, and I tried to explain to him what the difference could be, and I couldn't even put it into words. Somewhere in my upbringing, my [mind] knows the difference, somehow. I don't know if I was taught it, [or] if I learned it. How did I even come about to know the difference between an ache and a throb? And he doesn't have that perception. Pain is hard for him to describe, because—I don't want to say he doesn't feel it, because I think he feels pain—he just can't put it into the kind of language that we do.

And another thing: I needed to explain to him what it meant to be held against your will. Because there was an incident at school where he was talking to a girl, and I guess he must have put his hand up, because she wanted to go by, and he said, "No, I need to talk to you," and the girl got really upset. To her, he was making her stay there. And I sat with him on his bed, and I said, "Randy, you can never, ever hold anybody against their will." He didn't know what it meant. I remember, as soon as I said it, I looked at him, and I said, "Do you know what that means?", and he said no. Wow! So I sat there a minute, thinking, how do you explain to hold someone against their will? So I, kind of, just let that, kind of, go, and I said, "Well, let me think about it a bit, and tell me about your day at school." And I was sitting on his bed next to him, and while he was telling me about his classes and gym and what he did, I put my hand on top of his hand, rather firmly, and I didn't break eye contact. I said, so what happened after that, da, da, da, you know, we were talking, and after about, maybe, five or six seconds, I could feel he was uncomfortable with me holding his hand there, and he began to try to move his hand, and as he did, I didn't stop talking to him, but I applied more pressure, again holding his hand somewhere he didn't want it to be. And finally he stopped talking, he looked at me, [and] he says, "Why are you holding my hand there?" And I said, "Oh, I'm holding your hand against your will. You want your hand to be somewhere else, but I'm not letting it." And somehow that made the connection. I said, "That's like what holding someone against their will is."

I find myself always trying to put things into a concrete way of understanding. And it's very draining, because, [for example,] it took me a little while to figure out how I was going to explain holding someone against their will in a way that he would under-stand, that would be concrete, and would be in a subtle way. And it stuck. He knows what it means now. He understands the concept, and he was able to put it together. A lot of their acting inappropriately, I think, comes from the fact that they don't understand and they can't communicate the way we do.

He [also] takes expressions literally. One time, when he was eight, maybe nine years old, we were going to the store, and we were late, and I said, "Randy, hurry up. Quick, get your coat. Step on it." I went in his room, and there was his jacket on the floor, and he was stepping on it, and, of course, I lost it: "What are you doing?" And he said, "Hurry up, quick, get your coat, let's step on it," and he was serious.

So I'm really careful I don't say, "Randy, grab the cat, and throw him downstairs, so he doesn't go outside." Because he would grab the cat and throw him downstairs, and he has. I had a friend come to visit, and it was in the evening, and she went to use the bathroom, and she couldn't find the light. So she's in there going, "Tammy, where's the light?" And Randy walked by and said, "On the ceiling." He's right. I knew she meant the switch. [I would have said,] "It's on the right there, just put your hand around the corner." You know, he's very literal.

If we're out somewhere and I know he's heard an expression, I'll ask him, "Do you know what that means?", and he'll say no. And I'll say, if you ever hear that again, that's what it means. It doesn't mean what they're saying, it really means this. So again, I'm explaining a lot to him.

When he calls me on the telephone and I know he's going to call me on the telephone—you know, [if I tell him,] "Call me when the movie's over, I'll come and pick you up,"—he'll say, "Hi, Mom, this is your son, Randy Sherman." No kidding. I think that greeting is a carryover from church. We're very involved in church, and he goes there often.

[Another problem he has sometimes is] fitting the emotion to the event. He didn't understand when a grandmother died that we weren't close to, and we were at the wake, and I tried to prepare him for it, you know. I said, "We're going, and Meme will be in the casket, and you need to go up and just look and turn around to everyone that's in line there, Gramps and whoever, and shake their hand and just look at them and say, 'I'm sorry'." It was funny: he says, "Why do I have to say I'm sorry? I didn't kill her." I said, well, why are we sorry? I had to look at it, too, what we were doing, you know, and I said, "Maybe you're right, Randy. I guess we say we're sorry that they're sad. We're sorry that they're sad that their mother died, you know, that's what were sorry for." But I didn't think he could be sorry for that. That's something I could relate to, but it was beyond him.

When my husband died, when Randy's father died, Randy did not go to the wake. He was seven, and he only had been speaking about a year and not complete sentences yet. My husband dropped dead in our bathroom at home at midnight. So the children saw him. He had come home from work; he was 38. He had come home from a business meeting, and he felt sick, and he dropped dead in the bathroom. The children were small, and they saw it. I got back from the hospital, and my sister had taken the children, and I told them that Daddy was dead, and I told Randy that he would never see him again. And then he asked where he was, and I said, in Heaven, and he said he didn't see the rocket ship, and I told him that Jesus had come and carried him, and that was all that was said. Mariann came to the wake with me and to the burial, but Randy didn't, because I felt, back then—I had said, "Daddy's dead, and you're never going to see him again," and then I'd take him and show him this dead Daddy. So Randy didn't go through all that.

About two or three years ago, it was on Memorial Day, and Randy had questions about Dad's death: "Did it hurt? What did he feel?" He started to cry. That was difficult (it's hard even now), but that was the first time he had real questions. He believes in heaven, and I don't believe he's afraid of death. This is through our religious training, and I think he has a very strong belief, and we've talked about it. [He's asked me,] "Why can't Jesus heal me?" [I've answered,] "He can, but I think, maybe, he's got other things he wants you to do, as a handicapped person. Maybe something else is going to happen, and you're going to help some other people like you."

We have a dog, but I don't think he has [any] real closeness to animals. He very rarely pets her. She licked his foot this morning when I was trying to look at the swelling and everything. That was just absolutely disgusting for him. It's like the desk and the kitchen chairs: it has no meaning. It's just an object that's in the house. Once in awhile he'll look at her and say, "She's so beautiful," and then that's it. But to touch her and pet her and cuddle or anything: definitely not. He does care for her, and he also cleans up the mess, so he does do the physical things, but its just not an emotional attachment.

[In terms of sexuality,] he [does] masturbate, [but] he does it in his room, and he always has tons of Kleenex. I make sure there's boxes and boxes of them. I don't think it's an issue or problem. It was just getting him to understand that there are certain rules, you know. You wash your sheets, and, you know, tissues go in the trash. He was using his socks for awhile. I didn't like that, [so I told him,] "Please use Kleenex, tube socks is not the place." This is difficult as a Mom to address. I think the only other thing that, at the time, was an issue, and maybe still is, at times, is the manner in which he does it. I wish he could find another way, because he rubs on his sheet on his stomach, and he has a sore on his penis from the rubbing, and I've asked him to use his hand and he doesn't seem to know how to do that and I'm not about to show him. So it's difficult. Randy needs hands-on [experience] to learn. You have to show him, and who in the world is going to show him that?

He's had sex education. He's always gotten an A. He's had it for many years. Every September or October, I sign the papers so the school can do the same thing. And so he knows all about that; he knows how it's done. Because of our religious beliefs, he also knows that this is something that is saved for marriage.

He is affectionate with me. I ask him if I can hug him. I don't just hug him, because I think sometimes it hurts. But I'll ask him, and he'll say yes, and he hugs me.

[He has a problem] traveling in a car if we're going someplace new, [someplace] that I haven't been before. He gets frantic about getting lost. Suppose we're traveling to Worcester, and I've got to find such-and-such a place, and I go, "Oh, God, I can't believe it, it's not down here." [He'll ask,] "Are we lost? Are we lost?" He starts to get very excited, very agitated, and he's done this often. [He'll ask,] "Why are we stopping?", [if I stop the car] because I think the street was back there. [He'll say,] "Are we lost?" You know, he's really frightened about it. I mean, his whole voice and his body language and everything [show fear].

I usually now prepare him ahead of time. And what I usually try to do, which makes more work for me, is, if it's someplace that I have to go that I've never been before, I will take a dry run, because when I have him in the car with me, I don't want to have to go through the hassle of him thinking we are lost and panicking. It's just better, even though it takes more time for me to find the place a day or two before, know exactly where I'm going to park, and [be able to do it without hesitation when he's with me,] because to have to handle him in that kind of a situation is real difficult, when you're driving in an area you're not familiar with, and he's off the wall.

I think being lost has a different meaning for him than it does for me [or you]. We can say, geez, we're lost, but we have the option that we can go to the gas station or the police station, or we'll stop and ask somebody, ask our way. It's not the end of the world. But for him, he has a different perception of it, and it's really traumatic for him. I don't quite understand how he sees [being] lost, but [being] lost is very difficult, I mean, he panics. He just starts shouting, and he's frightened, so frightened: "Are we going to find our way? How can this happen?" And that, of course, makes me nervous, because he's so upset. He'll continue to do it until I tell him he's making me crazy, and then I try to calm down and tell him again: Randy, we're not lost. We're just going to stop, and I'll ask the man, or I'll ask the policeman, or I'll ask the guy at the gas station, and we'll just turn around. You know I try to simplify it and let him see that it's not whatever it is that he thinks it is.

[He also has a hard time understanding money.] He's ridden his bike up to this little breakfast place; it's up by the skating ring. If he's going to breakfast, he'll take $7, and sometimes he'll spend $7 on breakfast, too. And that was hard to explain to him, [that just] because you've got $7 doesn't mean you have to spend $7. You're only taking this amount so you'll have enough.

I remember being with him in a restaurant. He was young, maybe seven or eight years old, and you know how they keep filling the water glass? Every time she filled it, he drank it, and he drinks everything down in one gulp. He must have had seven glasses of water before our meal came. And finally, [after] she filled it up again, he went, "Mom, do I have to drink it? I don't think I can drink again." And then I realized [what he was doing]. I said, "Randy, you don't have to drink it." Same thing with the money: because I gave him $7, he thought he had to use $7 for breakfast. The kid almost exploded, you know.

He doesn't control his own finances. I have legal guardianship of him. [When] his SSI check comes, I cash it, and I give him money in an envelope each week that he uses for school expenses, to go to the roller rink, for McDonald's, [and for] going out with the group. He has another envelope that is just for flying. It says on it *flying money,* [and he uses it] when someone calls, and they're renting an airplane. He's got to pitch in 25 bucks. Everything is in envelopes, labelled.

[He can be left on his own.] I went away this past weekend. We left Friday night, and he was home watching a video, and that was fine with him. It was Mother's Day. I [had] planned on staying home, but he wanted me to go to the lake, and he was upset that I wasn't going to the lake. So I said, I'm out of here. He said [that] it makes him feel like he lives on his own when I go away. So Friday night, he was on his own. Saturday morning, he was going flying with a friend from church, and on Saturday afternoon, I had my niece come over and take him out for a grinder and then to a movie. And then Sunday, my girlfriend was bringing him to church. He's not at a point I'd be able to [leave him by himself without someone checking in with him].

Treatment

He takes Tegretal; it's an anti-seizure medication. He takes 900 milligrams a day. He had abnormal EEG patterns, which almost pointed to temporal lobe epilepsy. If he forgets to take his medication, I know. I can tell by the way he's processing information. He's just a little more distant. I can actually see that it's taking him longer to process what I've been saying to him. It takes longer to answer me. He always takes longer [than other people] anyway, [when answering a] question. He either thinks about what he's going to say, or it just takes him that long for the question to get to where it goes [in his brain]. He seems to be able to focus better on the medication, so we keep him on it.

And foods have an effect on him. Milk tends to aggravate him and make him angry, and excessive bananas will make him moody. Food coloring and preservatives [make him] high as a kite. Fritos make a noise in his head that he can verbalize. He'll tell you his head is going "mmmm" again. [I'll ask him,] "Well, did you eat Fritos?" [He'll answer,] "Yeah," [and, of course, I'll say,] "That's what happens, Randy!" If I see him having an excess [amount of Fritos], I'll say, "Randy, you know, maybe you better lay off, because it kind of makes you agitated, and you don't need this," and he will. He won't argue with it. I noticed it when he was 10. I brought him down to a clinic in Connecticut, and they have an experimental-type research program going on, where they actually test people for allergies to good things, like bananas, good food. But for Randy, it's not really a good food. He came out having different reactions [than most people].

I have him take powdered vitamin C in a glass of juice or something. Vitamin C, for him, works as a kind of a calming-down [substance]. If he's really, really agitated and not open to discussing anything, then, you know, [I need to tell him,] "You need to take some vitamin C and go sit in your room for 15 or 20 minutes, and when you can calm down, tone down your voice, come out here, and we'll talk. Before then, I don't want to see your face." He takes a teaspoonful in a glass of water or juice. It seems to help him calm down. If it doesn't really help him to calm down, really actually do it, maybe [it works because,] mentally, it's something tangible, again, that he feels he can take, that's going to help him to get himself calmed down, so he can stop shouting, and we can start talking.

I always try to alert [professional people] ahead of time [about his condition]. Like even yesterday, I got the [x-ray] technician [off to] the side, and I explained to him that Randy was autistic and that he may have a little trouble understanding. [Then] I went in there with him. They wanted his toes toward him, so they pulled his foot up towards him. Well, if someone did that to you, you would just keep it like that. Randy put his toes back down, and so I said to him, "Randy, he wants your foot like that, pull you toes toward your nose." But they were very nice to him, very kind and very soft spoken, once I told them.

Randy doesn't look unwell, and so they just thought, in fact, they looked at me like: what's this mother doing with this 22-year-old kid? So I explained it to them, and I tried to do it where he couldn't hear me, because it's embarrassing for him, you know.

When he was much younger, it would take, like, 4 or 5 visits to get a cleaning done [at the dentist's], because we couldn't get him to sit long enough to do everything in one procedure, you know. Now he is able to sit through it.

I think he received an adequate education. They focussed a lot on the positive things in life and tried as hard as they could to find a job placement for him, to sort out what he was good at and what he was bad at. As part of school, he did janitorial things, he worked at a nursing home to see how he did in food services. [His education was,] academically, you know, adequate. I don't think they wasted a lot of time on the things that Randy would never be able to achieve, which was good.

Stresses on the Family

I think something that, maybe, is worth mentioning is [that] Randy is 22, so I've been dealing with this for a long time. Of course, our medical field has changed a lot since Randy was a baby, but there was a point, when Randy was about a year and a half to two years old, that I was investigated for child abuse because of Randy's slow progress and seemingly mentally retarded condition. I would hope that today's medical profession would be a little less likely to look at the parent as the cause.

Randy had been hospitalized for about 17 days, for vomiting and pernicious dehydration, which he had gotten often, and while he was in the hospital, apparently, it seems like someone had called the hospital to say that I was locking Randy in closets for long periods of time. Randy was adopted, and the neighborhood wasn't too receptive to an adopted child. It was different back then.

The doctor had asked the visiting nurses association to come in and do an investigation, and when Randy was released, the doctor told me Randy had been very sick, and if I didn't mind, he'd ask a nurse to stop by the house occasionally, just to check on his progress and make sure he was recovering well.

Now, mind you, I was still back at the point where there was something wrong with my baby and no one believed me, so I was delighted to think that this nurse was going to come to my house and check on the baby, and maybe she would see something wrong with the baby, and then someone would believe I had a sick child. [This might have happened,] except the woman would show up unannounced, all hours of the day and night. I mean, she was just at my door, and she would come in, she would look to see what Randy was doing, she would stay, maybe, 10 or 15 minutes, and she would leave.

I was 23-24 years old, again, wanting someone to see that there was something wrong with my baby. I was just very happy to see her, and I never thought anything suspicious about it, until I requested medical records, to bring them with me to a doctor's visit, when he was about eight years old, and I had them in the house for the weekend and started reading them, and lo and behold, there it was, in black and white.

You know, the unfortunate thing was, the investigation was completed by this visiting nurse, but the medical record was never updated. In other words, there was no finality to the record. Nowhere in the record did they say, the investigation was completed on such-and-such a date, mother and father found to be adequate and loving parents. It was just this open thing. The problem, too, was [that] I had released his medical records to numerous places, because, as I sought help for Randy, and they asked, "Was he at another hospital?" I said yes. They asked, "Would you sign a release for the records?" Boom, they got the records, boom, they read this, and the next thing I knew they were asking my husband and me to come for counseling. Now it makes sense. Needless to say, I went back to the doctor, with an attorney, and demanded that he, at least—they cannot delete a medical record—add an amendment to it, which is in there now, on page skaty-eight, instead of, say, page 4, but it's in there.

It's very unfortunate, because I always feel, looking back, that [at] a lot of places we went to for help for Randy, they didn't get past that. And to this day, I feel like that hampered my getting help for Randy, because they kept looking at my husband and myself, rather than looking at him.

It's hard to say what effect Randy had on my family. I can't really speak for Mariann. I'm sure [that], if you sat and spoke with her, she would see it entirely different than I did. I like to think she wasn't denied any of my attention or anything, because that makes me feel good. When I'm really realistic about it, I would say it had to have affected her. There had to have been those times, when Mariann needed attention and needed me for whatever, that Randy also needed me, but he was not well, he was a sick child, and I would give him the attention. It makes sense, even though I can't recall anything, and it almost hurts a little to think that maybe she was neglected a little. But she had to be, it's logical.

Mariann and Randy got along really well, and she was really, really good with him. I thought she really understood him, and she was a big help with him, and she was very protective of him. And a lot of his acceptance at church came from the fact that Mariann acted like a buffer between Randy and his peers, to try and make them understand how Randy was, kind of paving the way for him, so everyone understood her brother.

[At one point,] we were all set to adopt another child. We had a phone call to tell us that we would have a child within two weeks, [but] I had taken Randy up to the mental health clinic, and they told me I had a very sick child, and I called up the agency and said we can't take this—it was going to be a mixed race baby—and I told then we just couldn't, that Randy was going to take everything, all my time, everything I had.

I keep [my relationships with men and Randy] separate. I don't put us all together. John and I have been going out for almost 4 years, but we don't do anything as a family. We don't go out, John and Randy and me. I go out with John or I'm out with Randy; I don't put it all together. Because I find, if I put us all together, I'm in the middle, [between] John who wants my attention and Randy who needs my attention, and I'm not going to put myself in there. I'm not going to do that. John is very good to Randy, and Randy is very indifferent to John, but Randy is very indifferent to a lot of people. They exist within an area together. They communicate: "Hi, how are you?" "Good, how are you?" "Good." And that's it. I would like to get married, I would. It [just] doesn't make sense if Randy is still with me. It wouldn't work with all of us together, it just wouldn't.

Long Range Forecast

He's graduating from high school on the 30th of this month, and [then] he's done with school, period. The state only educates to [age] 22. I guess they can't stay in school forever. He does have an 8-10 week, part-time job at Friendly's, sorting mail. He's been doing that [job] right along, as part of his school program, anyway. I spoke with them yesterday. He's going to be working Monday, Wednesday, and Friday, for 5 hours, for minimum wage. [It's] the same job that he's been doing as part of school. And what I'm hoping is, after the 8-10 weeks is up, maybe they'll extend it. There's a supervisor there who's been training him. I hope this works.

He's been fired from jobs in the past. He was bagging at a supermarket as part of school. And then, when school was out for the summer, they kept him on for 6-7 hours a week. And they kept telling me he wasn't doing well. When school was in session, the teacher or one of the aides would go over [with him], but once school was out, there wasn't [anyone to go with him].

They said his problem was that he would stay at the same register, and registers on both sides would have tons of groceries and need a bagger, but he couldn't make that conscious [decision, couldn't think] that, I need to move to that register and bag there now, because no one is in this line. They were very aggravated that they constantly had to tell him, "Randy, bag for her now. Randy, bag for her now." I couldn't understand how he could possibly be having trouble bagging. It's so simple. So I got him a job at another supermarket, and they were going to give him more hours a week. They were going to give him, like, 15 hours a week, and they were very open to him. So he started working there, and he really was having problems, and unfortunately, there wasn't the communication. They didn't call me, because, if they had, I could have worked it through with them. He was having problems bagging. He was getting annoyed with the customers. I think, again, it was moving from place to place. What got him fired was [an incident when] a big order had come, and it was, like, a whole bunch of separate orders, even though she was paying all together, and it was one of these: I want this and this and this in that kind of bag and that in this bag; no, no, no, this goes in this bag . . . . And it was confusing, and he just threw his hands up in the air, and he said, "Bag it yourself," and he walked away. And that's what he'll do, he will walk away from a situation. And that was it, they called me and told me they were having problems and to come and get Randy. And, boy, I was very angry with him, because, number one, I felt that he had been rude to the customer. You don't throw your hands up in the air and tell someone to bag it yourself, it's rude. So I was real angry with him for a couple of days, for being fired, and because I thought he didn't handle it right.

A couple of days later, we were talking about it more, and he said, "Ma, it's confusing, it's confusing. Don't you understand? It's confusing, bagging." [I said,] "My God, what's confusing? You take the groceries, you open the stupid bag, you put the stupid groceries in the stupid bag and put it in the carriage, and the person goes away. What do you mean, confusing?" And he said, "Ma, [you have to] put this in this kind of bag, this in this kind of bag. Everything is always different. Every grocery order was different." So it was like asking Randy to learn a new job every time someone new came to the register. In my mind, it was simple: you take the stupid groceries, and you put them in the stupid bag, but for Randy, it was never [simple]. If it was always meat and potatoes, a gallon of milk, it would have been fine.

And he started crying, just [saying], "It was confusing, so confusing. Isn't it confusing for you?" And I said, "No, Randy, it's not, but my brain's different than your brain. Okay, now I understand. But you still shouldn't have shoved the lady's bags. That was rude. You don't talk like that to people. So he got fired. So now I know that bagging, as simple as bagging is, it's not simple for Randy.

But, from what I understand, he is fantastic at sorting the mail. They tell me there's over 500 mail boxes, and he sorts them as accurately and as quickly as everybody normal in the whole place.

I'm trying to link up with agencies [that offer] supportive services. There are agencies out there to serve all kinds of people with illnesses, drug addiction, and alcohol addiction, and there is nothing to serve the autistic adult who isn't mentally retarded. And that's what I'm mad about. If he were mentally retarded, he would be served by the Department of Mental Retardation and have bussing and have all kinds of programs, but because he's not mentally retarded, there are no services for Randy. [Society's attitude is:] Mom, you find him a job; Mom, you take care of him; Mom, you transport him. That's why I have an attorney. Something is wrong with the picture. If he were a drug addict, he would be in a rehabilitation program tomorrow, with all kinds of support. The only times I've thought that maybe I didn't do the right thing are when I'm denied services for him because he's not handicapped enough, and I say, maybe I didn't do him such a favor. If I had left him twittering and chirping and clucking, he'd be eligible for everything under the sun, but because I wouldn't allow him to stay in that place, did I really do this kid a favor?

He falls through the cracks and was denied [services] because his IQ was not 70. That's why we're appealing, with the use of an attorney. His IQ's gone anywhere from 77 to 83. I think Randy is setting a precedent, and I think that this has happened for a reason. I think that everyone wants to get [the definition of mental retardation] changed [to something other than an IQ score of 70 or less. But] it's making my life miserable, big time! What's really nice, [though,] is [that] the Department of Mental Retardation on the local level here is 100% on our side. They want to serve Randy. They called me last week and told me that they will serve Randy for respite care after July 1, because he will no longer be eligible under Community Resources for People with Autism, because they only go up to [age] 22.

A week ago, in the Sunday paper, there was something about a state-mandated van service for the handicapped. So I called them the very next morning, and I got the application, but again it's, like, yes-and-no answers. Can you wait for a bus for more than 10 minutes? Today, yes; tomorrow, maybe no. You know, for Randy, it's a hard thing to say. Can you ride a taxi? He's done it. Can he do it consistently? Probably not. If the bus was supposed to come at 10 and it never showed up at 10 o'clock, he would still stand there waiting for the bus, because he doesn't have the ability to say, oh, I've been here three hours, maybe I better call Mom, or maybe I better walk home, or maybe I better do something about it.

My goal for him is [that] I want him out of my home. He needs to be out of my home. [The] bottom line [is that] I am not going to live forever, and I tell Randy, "Randy, someday, when I'm dead, you are going to have to know how to do this." When he hurt his ankle, I stayed home from work, iced it, elevated it, gave him his medicine, for one whole day. The next day I said, "Now you do it yourself." [He asked,] "Aren't you going to do it for me?" [I said,] "No, Randy, you saw how it was done yesterday. You do it now, because someday I am going to be dead, and you are going to have to do this yourself." And I tell him that, over and over again. I say it once or twice or week: "Someday, Randy I'm not going to be here, I'm going to be dead." It's concrete. It sounds awful and cruel, but there's no mincing words with him. He's got the message: you have to know how to do this yourself.

I was hoping this last winter to put my house on the market. My idea is, Randy and I both hate winter, so I want to move to Florida. In Florida I could afford two homes. I could see Randy in one of these mobile home parks where they're all stationary—you know, they're just like houses—where it's quieter and calmer and a little bit protected. In his own little mobile home, and I would be in the same park, or across the street. I could afford two mobile homes. I could probably afford a mobile home and a small home in Florida, and that's what my idea is. He would be with me at first, he would live in my home, just as he does now. But in the end I would purchase a small home for him right in walking distance and put him in it and teach him how to live in it, [how to] get his groceries and shop and pay his bills with his check and live on the extra money, and then, when I am dead, hopefully he can carry on with it.

He says, I want to get married someday, I want to have children, I want to be a pilot, blah, blah, blah. And I said to him, "Randy, you have difficulty taking care of yourself, you know. A baby doesn't know anything." I tried to explain to him that you have to think for the child, and if you can't make rational decisions for yourself, how are you going to for the baby? And would you want to take the chance of having a child that might be autistic or have brain damage or go through the difficult times that you've gone through? And most of the times that ends the conversation. He doesn't want to talk about it anymore. He just shuts down.

Social Stigma

Now he's beginning to understand that [he sometimes acts] strange, and I do remind him. Like this morning, he decided to wait at the bus stop with the other kids. He hasn't been all winter, but it's warm enough, and I said, "Randy, remember to watch how you're acting out there," and I know that he understood [that] what I meant was, please don't act like a weirdo, because these kids are going to make fun of you, and he doesn't like it when he's made fun of. And yet he initiates so much of it himself. [For example,] he'll pace and talk to himself. So we're trying to make him really aware of how he's presenting himself. He definitely can control it, [but] when I've asked him, "Randy, when are you going to stop doing that?", [he's said,] "Maybe tomorrow." [If I ask,] "Why don't you do it today?", [he'll answer,] "I can't today, but maybe tomorrow."

A mistake he did make was when he was at the roller rink. A girl was there selling candy bars for school, and he bought all of them. She had fifteen, and they were a dollar each, and he bought them all. He doesn't even eat candy bars. I think she took advantage of him. So I explained to him that was not to be done. You can buy one or two. Again, I have to put it, you may only buy two, because if I said a couple, that's not specific enough.

Surviving and Transcending

[The way I cope is:] I take one Xanax at bedtime, and I get a good night's sleep. And if I get a good night's sleep, I can handle pretty much everything during the day. And that's truly how I handle it. And I cry, and I get angry, and then I pick myself up, and I brush myself off, and I just do it. I don't know, sometimes, how I do it. People say they don't know how I do it. I don't know; there's something inner, inside, I find. I pray. I get mad at God too.

[I've gotten outside counseling, but not for help in dealing] with Randy. I did after my husband died, but I never felt I needed it to deal with Randy. Maybe I [can] deal with him [on my own] because I get the outside help for the other issues. And that allows me space to deal with him.

I think part of my attitude towards Randy, what, maybe, makes it easy for me, is the fact that he's not my birth child. I carry no guilt whatsoever. Because I've talked to a lot of parents with autistic or handicapped children, and one thing I pick up right away is [that] they feel guilty, because they produced a child that is not well, not normal, and they carry along [this guilt], like, on their shoulder, just dragging it along, and I have none of that. I think, in a way, that has enabled me to do a lot more for Randy.

Also, he has a wonderful perspective. We were having dinner at a little Italian restaurant, and he asked me—he asks me periodically questions about his birth mother; doesn't mention his birth father, but he has asked questions about his birth mother—and he asked me, one day, he said—I don't know how we were on the subject, or where it came up, but he just asked me about my being pregnant with my daughter—[he said,] "Mariann was born in 1966, so you got pregnant in 1966. And I said, "No, Randy, I got pregnant in 1965. Mariann was born in 1966, because it takes nine months to have a baby." And he said, "So my—what do you call that lady?" And I said, "Your birth mother." [And he asked,] "When did she get pregnant with me?" And I said, "Probably 1969, and you were born in 1970." And he said, "That was nice of them to do that." And it was just so sweet. It was just so precious, because [he was saying,] if she didn't get pregnant for me, I wouldn't have been here. "That's nice of them to do that." And I thought, oh, my God.

It was beautiful, you know, and I was tapping myself on the

shoulder, saying, here's a kid that's not saying, my mother didn't love me, my birth mother gave me away, and feeling, maybe, all that kind of stuff that, maybe, some adopted children might feel, thinking they were abandoned or unloved. And here he's happy he was born. "That's nice of them to do that." I couldn't believe it; it was so precious. And I patted myself on the shoulder, I really did. I said, you know, Tammy, somewhere along his upbringing, you never let him feel like she and he, whoever they are, didn't love him or didn't do something good for him. Once in a while, he comes out with something real sweet like that.

This is who he is, and I feel very good about how far I have brought him. I feel like I am being selfish and blowing my own horn, but I've worked like hell for that kid, and I see it. I see it all the time. He's not anywhere near as handicapped as they all said he would be. [They said] that he'd never be anybody or anything and I should put him away. I was told to institutionalize him when he was three or four, and probably again when he was seven or eight. I got him out of an institution, I got him out of the orphanage, there's no way I would put him back! And then it almost made me so angry that it was almost [like I felt]: oh, yeah, well, I'll show you, watch me. And that's what I did. It just gave me that little kick more that I needed, and that was it, and it has never let up. And look at what I did, and, darn, I feel good about it.

Chapter 8
Summary and Comments

This book has offered two perspectives on the subject of how parents experience autism in their children. The first is an empirical, scientific perspective, which objectively documents the demands placed on these parents. The second is a subjective, personal perspective from the parents themselves, which encourages us to empathize with their predicament. It should come as no surprise that, approaching this issue from these two perspectives, we reach similar conclusions, since empirical investigations are based on real-life cases. This overlap, however, functions in two ways: The scientific findings legitimize the parental laments, and the parents' stories humanize the scientific data.

What is Autism?

Although autism manifests itself in many different ways, the three core themes from DSM-IV (impairment in social interaction, impairment in communication, and the presence of idiosyncratic behaviors) are evident in each of the 6 cases presented in this volume. In addition, each child has additional problems not specifically addressed in DSM-IV.

To begin with, all six children have clear problems with social interaction. All the children relate to others with affection, but only when the contact is initiated by others. Most engage in solitary activity, which is a source of pleasure for each of them, but have no friends their own age. For most of the children, adult contact is self-serving. The younger children are not interested in toys, or prefer toys that are for children younger than themselves. Family pets are, for the most part, ignored.

Impairment in communication is also evident. Two of the children have very limited speech. The more verbal children have problems with perseveration on certain phrases or topics. They also use words and phrases they don't understand and have trouble with more abstract concepts, such as figurative expressions. One child enjoys making up words, although many of them are nonsensical.

A number of the children have motor stereotypies involving waving or flapping their fingers or arms, rocking, playing with threads, or pacing. Many of them have obsessional interest in certain objects, such as glass, elevators, or windshield wipers, or in activities, such as watching certain videotapes. Those with obsessional interests are resistant to change. At least two of the children show prodigious memories, but it appears that they don't fully understand what they have memorized.

Lastly, all the children have other serious associated behaviors. A number of the children have sleep disturbances. Two of the children are incontinent at night, and one has had problems with smearing feces. Safety is an issue with almost every child, especially when crossing streets. Daily living skills, such as personal grooming, are more of a problem for the younger children, although the older children sometimes need prompting as well. Emotional responses are restricted, as in the case of grief, or inappropriate, as in the case of laughter. Aggressive behavior toward others, including physical aggression and verbal threats, is present in some of the children, as is self-injurious behavior. However, only one of the six cases has a serious problem with self-injurious behavior. Sexuality is a concern for half of the parents; the other children seem to show no interest. Some of the older children are aware they have a disability, but are not fully aware of their limitations, as evidenced by their sometimes unrealistic desires of the moment and dreams for the future.

Difficulties with Diagnosis

The five parents who have been with their child from infancy all suspected from early in their child's life that something was seriously wrong, only to have their pediatricians tell them to wait it out and not overreact. Only at the parents' insistence were specialists seen, at first, usually, speech therapists or neurologists, and later on, mental health professionals. In many cases, years went by before a definitive diagnosis was made. Many parents admitted having been angry at the time of diagnosis with their doctors for a variety of reasons, including: they were looking for someone to blame; they felt their doctors had acted insensitively (e.g., giving them a diagnosis over the phone); their doctors had offered them little hope; they had implied that the parents were ignorant of the normal range of maturation rates in children; or they had suggested that the parents had contributed to their child's condition.

Confusion Over Labelling

The children were initially labelled as having special needs, being developmentally delayed, or having autistic-like behavior. One of the older boys was, at first, said to have childhood schizophrenia. Later on, the children were labelled as having autism.

Although all parents are correctly aware that their child has a biological disorder of the brain, even if it has not been detected physically, at least one parent is confused about the distinction between physical and mental disorders and between autism and mental retardation. The problem of the word *autistic* sometimes meaning withdrawn also made parents initially question the diagnosis.

Unanswered Questions of Cause

In two of the cases, complications were present during pregnancy that could have caused the autistic disorder, specifically toxemia and a high fever. In three of the other cases, there were problems at birth or shortly thereafter, including a long labor and breech birth, a post-date delivery followed by an infection, and absence of a fetal heart beat during labor. In the remaining case, there was no problem with either the pregnancy or the delivery, and this parent attributes the autism disorder to a possible genetic predisposition. In each case, however, the parents can only speculate as to the cause of the autism.

Grief and Sorrow

Both husbands and wives, typically, first responded to the autism diagnosis with prolonged crying. Some parents talk about the need to mourn the loss of a child who never was and having to bond with a new child. After a period of time, the grief seems contained, only to return at marker occasions, such as holidays, vacations, or having to seek guardianship.

Trials of Day-to-Day Living

Although all the children have the number and type of symptoms characteristic of autism, some problems are more trying than others on a day-to-day basis. Many parents are forced to be constantly vigilant by the combination of their child having less or, seemingly, no sensitivity to pain and being oblivious to danger. One boy requires medical attention for his self-abusive behavior. Three children are also capable of being seriously aggressive to others.

Other problems are more exasperating to parents than serious. These include such behaviors as talking to oneself, laughing inappropriately, pacing, masturbating in public, inconsolable tantrums, lengthy verbal perseverations, and obstinateness. And for a number of parents, their children's difficult behaviors do not let up during the night time hours, so they have had to learn to cope with a difficult situation on a daily basis with very little sleep.

Trying to Get Adequate Treatment

All of the children live at home and attend school during the week. For the children with the greatest needs, the programs are separate special education classes. For the children with lesser needs, a combination of mainstreaming with an aide present and special classes are used. For most of the older children, a vocational program is incorporated into their school activities.

Parents whose children have moved from special education with other special needs children to mainstreamed classes, where their child is the only special needs child, feel their child's behavior improved after the move and attribute this to the fact that their children now have normal children as models.

The two children who are the least verbal are involved with facilitated communication, a technique considered, by most professionals in this field, to have questionable validity. One mother believes in its efficacy and is amazed at how capable her daughter appears while facilitating with her teachers, although she laments that her daughter does not do as well with her. The alleged success, however, does not appear to contribute to improvement in her overall behavior. The other parent is much more skeptical and feels that she and the other facilitators are mostly influencing the outcome. Also, she feels that this technique does not help her son with functional behaviors and that that's what he is most in need of developing.

The children are taught by either special education teachers or regular teachers. None of the teachers appears to have been trained primarily in autism, nor are they behavioral specialists, although the schools do use consultants and outside specialists. In one case, a parent hired a behavioral consultant, but felt the techniques were not applicable to her son. The type of reinforcers suggested, which might have been reinforcing for most other children, were clearly not reinforcing to her son, so she stopped using them. Unfortunately, other reinforcers were not suggested or explored.

Three of the children are on medication. Two are taking Haldol for behavioral management, and one is taking Tegretal for seizures. These parents feel their children have shown noticeable improvement while on these medications.

Stresses on the Family

All of the parents are either married and living with their spouses or in long-term relationships, and all report satisfaction with their partners and with their partners' relationships to their children, although, in some cases, the partners' relationships to the children are limited.

The parents of the younger children with autism talk about how consuming the disorder is and how difficult it is to find adequate respite care. The married parents of the older children talk about the difficulty or impossibility of taking vacations, especially alone as a couple. The two parents who are not married try to protect private time with their partners by keeping some separation between the partners and the children with autism.

All the parents have concerns over the effect their children with autism have had on their other children. In the cases where the siblings are older than the child with autism, the parents worry about having short-changed the older child, in terms of attention, and about the older child having had to grow up too fast. In the cases where the siblings are younger, the parents worry about the normal child copying the unusual behaviors of the child with autism, about the normal child's fear of developing autistic symptoms, and about the normal child being a target for the aggression of the child with autism.

A number of parents have decided not to have other children because they are worried about a possible hereditary cause, and many voice concerns over the chance that their grandchildren might one day be afflicted.

Uncertain Long Range Forecast

All six children still live at home, but all the parents have hopes that they will someday be able to live in a group home or other supervised environment.

While the parents of the two youngest children are still very unsure of what the future holds for their children, the parents of the older children have a sense of what type of work will be most suitable for their children, and two of the older children already have part-time jobs as part of their high school curriculum. Two of the older children have career aspirations which, unfortunately, are not realistic, given the limits on their abilities. Also, two of the older children indicate a desire to get married, and one wants to have children, although these goals seem very unlikely for the near future.

Two parents have children over 18 years old. In one case, the parent experienced difficulty getting guardianship, in part because her son was on medication. The other parent did not have any difficulty getting guardianship, but is having difficulty obtaining services, such as respite, for her son, because his IQ is just above the cutoff for mental retardation.

Social Stigma

All the parents report that people stare at their children in public places, but that it does not usually prevent them from taking their children with them.

The older children are more likely to be harassed when they are alone with their peers at school. The harassment includes name-calling, shouting of obscenities, mocking, teasing, threats, and physical abuse. Some children are also taken advantage of financially. Some parents, justifiably incensed by this treatment, have come close to inflicting harm on the harassers.

Surviving and Transcending

These parents survive and transcend their experience in many ways. They have learned to accept in themselves a range of powerful emotions, such as grief and anger. They have also learned to habituate, to adopt a positive attitude, and to use humor, religion, respite help, support groups, and the support of caring friends and family. They have a persistent, dogged dedication to improving life for their children. They speak of a special bond with their children, and they take great pride in both their children's hard-won accomplishments and their own contributions to those accomplishments. They are also proud that their children have attained greater goals than they had expected them to or had been led to believe they could.

Rather than becoming embittered, the parents talk about how they have become better people for having had a child with autism. They see their own development in two areas: they are more confident, better able to handle crises, and better able to voice their needs and get them met, and they are more sensitive, loving, and tolerant of others, and have a greater appreciation of life in general.

Conclusion

Although no one who is not the parent of a person with autism can ever know the full extent of the experience, it is hoped that, through presenting these two perspectives on autism, the parents' experience is more understandable to those who will never face the challenge of raising a child with autism. It is also hoped that, in reading this book, the parents of children with autism will feel recognized for their extraordinary experience.

It is also hoped that this work will stimulate some ideas for research into prevention and treatment, so that the battle with autism may someday be won. The needs are many and obvious; unfortunately, the solutions are not. We need to develop earlier and better means of diagnosing this disorder, including genetic screening techniques and counseling. We need more aggressive research on the medical treatment of autism, including better medications and, perhaps, even more radical types of experimentation, such as tissue implantation. We need to subdivide the different manifestations of autism and provide sound prognoses and educational options. We need to develop more programs to train educators to work with individuals with autism, and to pay these educators the salaries they deserve. We need to provide structured respite services away from home. We need to develop better programs to assist adult individuals with autism to live independently. Lastly, and most importantly, we need to listen and provide more support to the courageous families whose lives have been immeasurably affected by this demanding and debilitating disorder called autism.

APPENDIX A

PARENTS' QUESTIONNAIRE

Background

What is the name of your child with autism?

What is your child's date of birth?

Who else is living with you and your child?

How old are they, and what are their relationships to your child?

Does your child have any other brothers or sisters?

Where are they living, and what are their ages?

(If not living with the child) Where are your child's biological mother and father, and what contact do they have with their child?

When did you first suspect something with wrong with your child?

What made you think that?

What professional did you first consult regarding your child?

What did this professional tell you?

Did you see any other professionals regarding your child?

If so, what did they say?

When were you first told your child was autistic?

Did you know what that meant?

Had you previously known anyone with this disorder?

If so, was the person in your family or outside of your family?

What was your reaction to being told your child was autistic?

What was your spouse's reaction?

What was your family's reaction?

What do you think caused your child to be autistic?

Daily Life

Think about a typical Saturday or Sunday for your child, or any day s/he would be spending mostly with you. Describe it in detail. Pay particular attention to things your child does that would be considered unusual for a child of his or her age, or that are difficult to deal with.

What about your child's sleeping arrangements?

Does your child have any bed time rituals?

Does your child wear pajamas to bed?

Can your child go to bed by himself or herself?

Does your child sleep alone?

What time does your child go to bed?

For how many hours does your child sleep?

Does your child ever get up in the middle of the night?

If so, what does your child do then?

Has your child ever told you that s/he has had a dream or nightmare, or acted as though s/he has had one?

Does your child have any other problems sleeping?

What time does your child wake up?

How does your child wake up (e.g., alarm clock)?

What is your child's state when first waking up?

What are the first things your child does when s/he wakes up?

Does your child pick out what clothes s/he will wear for the day?

Are there any peculiarities in what your child wants to wear?

Does your child resist having his or her clothes changed?

Can your child dress himself or herself?

Can your child groom himself or herself (e.g., bathe or shower, shave, wash hair, apply deodorant, deal with menstruation, or brush hair)?

Can your child toilet himself or herself?

Does your child have any issues around privacy (yours or the child's)?

What about meals?

What will your child eat and drink for breakfast?

What won't they eat or drink for breakfast?

Are there any breakfast rituals you have to follow?

What happens if you don't?

Can your child keep himself or herself clean while s/he eats (e.g., use as napkin)?

Does your child leave a mess after eating (e.g., crumbs on the floor)?

Can your child use a knife to cut food?

Can your child prepare any foods unassisted?

What about lunch: are there any rituals or special foods for this meal?

What about dinner (supper)?

What does your child do?

Can your child occupy himself or herself?

Does your child play with his or her brothers and sisters?

Does your child have any friends?

What are your child's biggest interests?

Does your child help around the house?

Does your child do any chores?

Does your child have any favorite objects?

Does your child enjoy spinning things?

Does your child like windshield wipers?

Does your child like playing with water?

Does your child like receiving presents?

Does your child watch television?

If so, does s/he have any favorite shows?

Does your child have any unusual interests?

Does your child have any unusual talents (e.g., memory, art, music, or calendar calculating)?

Does money have any meaning to your child?

Does your child ever use money independently to buy things?

What is your child's speech like today?

Can you understand your child's speech?

Can strangers understand it?

Does your child ever mutter to himself or herself?

If so, how often?

Does your child ever repeat himself or herself?

If so, what does your child say and how often?

Does your child have some phrases s/he says all the time (e.g., "I don't care")?

Does your child ever just repeat what you have said?

Does your child ever tell the same stories over and over again, without any recognition that s/he has told you the story already?

Does your child make up words or say unusual things?

Does your child ever switch pronouns (e.g., say you for I)?

Does your child ever start to talk about something without introducing the topic first?

Does your child ever persist in talking even when you say you have already heard that?

Is the quality of your child's voice unusual (e.g., higher than normal, singsong, or monotonous)?

Can your child understand expressions or jokes?

Does your child look at you while you are talking to him or her and while s/he is talking to you?

How does your child greet people s/he knows?

What does your child do when introduced to strangers?

Does your child ever use gestures or facial expressions to communicate?

If so, is there anything unusual about these?

Has your child ever used sign language or a language board?

Does your child ever write to communicate?

Can your child read?

If so, at what age level does s/he read?

Does your child understand what s/he is reading?

Does your child seem more sensitive to sensory stimuli than normal (e.g., noise or bright lights), or less sensitive to other stimuli (e.g., pain)?

Is there anything of a sensory nature that your child really likes or dislikes?

What are your child's emotions like?

Is your child affectionate with you, with other family members, or with strangers?

Does your child ever show inappropriate emotions (e.g., laugh or giggle at something serious)?

Does your child ever cry inconsolably or for no apparent reason?

Are there things that your child is afraid of?

Are there things that make your child happy?

Does your child ever say s/he is happy, sad, afraid, etc.?

Are there any problems around sexuality (e.g., with masturbation or inappropriate talk)?

Is your child ever aggressive?

If so, is the aggression directed toward himself or herself or toward others?

What form does the aggression take (e.g., pinching, biting, poking, hitting or throwing things)?

Has your child ever hurt anyone seriously?

Is there anything you can do to control your child's aggression?

Does your child swear or curse?

How do you discipline or control your child?

How well does it work?

Have you ever tried to hit your child as a punishment?

If so, did your child hit back?

Do you use any techniques taught to you by a professional or teacher (e.g. schedules or reinforcements)?

Do you ever find yourself just giving in to your child?

If so, does this happen often?

Do you have any tricks you've learned to get your child to do certain things?

Is your child more or less active than a normal child of similar age?

Does your child engage in any odd behaviors, such as rocking, finger-gazing, or unusual walking (e.g., on the toes)?

How coordinated is your child?

Can your child catch a ball?

Is your child interested in physical activities?

Can your child swim?

Does your child have any physical problems in addition to autism (e.g., seizures)?

Is your child on any medication?

If so, what medication, and for what condition?

Does it help?

Have you tried other medications before?

What were the results?

What is your child like when s/he is sick (e.g., with a cold, flu, or fever)?

How does your child respond to doctors and dentists?

Do you have any pets?

What is your child's reaction to them?

How does your child respond to animals in general?

Where does your child go to school?

Is this a public or private school?

Is your child integrated into a regular class for any or all subjects?

What is the teacher/student ratio?

How many other kids with autism are there in your child's school?

Does your child go to summer school or camp?

What is your child's reaction to school (does s/he like it)?

Does what your child learns at school transfer to home?

Are there any special programs available to you that integrate school and home?

How difficult is it for you to teach your child something new?

How difficult is it for you to explain something to your child?

How well does your child respond to criticism, to being told something is wrong, or to being told that s/he can't do something?

Do other kids ever tease or make fun of your child, or call him or her names?

How does your child react?

Does your child see any specialists outside of school, such as a psychologist, psychiatrist, speech therapist, physical therapist, or religious leader?

What kind of judgment does your child show?

Does s/he ever do things that are unsafe, either for himself or herself or for
others?

Can your child describe himself or herself?

Does your child know s/he is autistic or different?

How is your child when riding in the car?

Does your child have any rituals for car travel?

Will your child wear a seatbelt?

Can you take your child out shopping or to restaurants?

Do you ever go to the movies with your child?

Does your child ever cause a scene in public?

If so, how do you deal with this?

How does it make you feel?

Have you ever felt that strangers were being judgmental towards you
because you were unable to control your child's behavior?

Have you ever gone on vacation with your child?

If so, where did you go and for how long?

Did you have any problems?

Do your neighbors know your child is autistic?

What is their reaction?

Do you ever have the feeling that your child is just being stubborn and that
s/he knows more than s/he lets on?

Do you get any help taking care of your child?

Do other members of your family help out?

Do you get any respite?

If so, how much?

What has that been like?

Do you have any other babysitters?

Do you have trouble finding people to care for your child?

Can your child ever be left alone?

If so, for how long?

What does your child do while alone?

What's the longest time you have been able to be away from your child?

Are you employed?

If so, full or part time?

What kind of work do you do?

Do you ever bring work home?

If so, how easy is it to work at home?

Do you think your child is getting better or worse over the years?

What was your child like when s/he was younger?

Attitudes

Are you bothered by your child's behavior?

What puzzles you most about your child?

What has been the hardest part of raising your child?

What has been the most rewarding part of raising your child?

Do you accept the fact that your child is different?

Do you compare your child to other kids his or her age?

Do you ever imagine what your child might have been like had s/he not been autistic?

Do you ever think about your child's future?

What do you think it will be like?

Do you think your child will be able to live away from you?

Do you think your child will be able to have a job?

Do you think your child will ever be able to drive a car?

Have you ever considered institutionalizing your child?

What effect has having a child with autism had on your life?

What effect has it had on your family?

What effect has it had on your marriage?

Has having a child with autism changed your mind about having other children?

Do you think your other children could have children with autism ?

Have you ever discussed this with them?

How do you cope with having a child with autism ?

Do you belong to any support groups?

Is there anyone else you get support from?

How much do you read about autism?

What advice you would give to people who just found out their child was autistic?

Is there anything else you'd like to talk about?

APPENDIX B

SUGGESTIONS FOR PARENTS

1. Become affiliated with the Autism Society of America (ASA). The national headquarters are located at 7910 Woodmont Avenue, Suite 650, Bethesda, MD 20814. Their main telephone number is 1-301-657-0881. In addition, they have a hotline at 1-800-3AUTISM and a fax number: 1-301-657-0869. This organization has over 200 state chapters. It publishes a magazine, *The Advocate*, which comes out six times a year and is free with membership. It also sponsors an annual 4-day conference on autism. The cost of membership in ASA is $20 for an individual and $30 for a family. To receive information on how to join, to find out the location of the nearest ASA chapter, to receive free information packets on various topics, or to ask for advice, call the hotline Monday through Friday from 9am to 5pm (ET).

Another organization that provides information packets to parents, as well as a diagnostic checklist, is the Autism Services Center, Pritchern Building, 607 North Street, Huntington, WV 25710, 1-304-525-8014.

A third source of basic information is the American Association of University Affiliated Programs for Persons with Developmental Disabilities (AAUAP), 8630 Fenton Street, Suite 410, Silver Spring, MD 20910, 1-301-588-8252. This organization is a network of 59 university-affiliated centers which diagnose and treat people with autism and other developmental disabilities.

Parents who want to talk directly to other parents of children with autism can do so via the Internet. One popular address is
AUTISM@SJUVM.STJOHNS.EDU.

2. Educate yourself about autism. I have often heard from parents of individuals with autism that so little is written about autism. Nothing could be further from the truth. For example, there were 1,922 articles written on autism in psychology journals between January, 1987 and November, 1994.Over this same period, there were 518 books or chapters in books written on the subject. (the number of articles and books or chapters written during this time on Pervasive Developmental Disorder was 98 and 18, respectively).

Every reference used in this book is listed here. To see the entire book or article, consult your librarian. Even if your local library does not have it, most librarians now have electronic access to the catalogues of other libraries, and most libraries have inter-library loan capabilities.

To keep abreast of the latest research, use professional computer databases, such as PsycInfo or MEDLINE (available at major colleges and universities), or order PsycSCAN_LD/MR, Abstracts on Communication Disorders and Mental Retardation, from the American Psychological Association, 750 First Street NE,

Washington, DC 20002 (subscription rate: $32 per year). These services will provide you with short summaries of recently published research on autism. If you want the entire article, again, ask your librarian for assistance.

The journal that publishes the most studies on autism is the *Journal of Autism and Developmental Disorders*, published by the Plenum Publishing Company, 233 Spring Street, New York, NY 10013 (individual subscription rate: $50 per year).

You may find that you have trouble understanding many of the articles written by professionals for professionals. Your physician, psychologist, or social worker may be able to help you translate them into common English.

There are also a number of videos available on autism. Research Press (Department N, Post Office Box 9177, Champaign, IL 61826) publishes a number of good ones, including *Parenting Children with Disabilities* and *Parents' Views of Living with a Child with Disabilities*. They will send you a complete catalog upon request. Some of the videos are expensive. In these cases, you might arrange for a school or ASA chapter to purchase them, or you might be able rent them from Research Press or by interlibrary loan from a college or university library.

3.   Find a way to express what is happening to you. Your local ASA chapter (see suggestion #1) should be able to recommend a support group. Consider seeing a psychotherapist, not because you have a psychological problem or are the source of your child's problem, but because you are under stress. Find a good friend who will listen and empathize with you. Keep a diary of your experiences.

4.   Find and use respite care on a weekly basis and for extended vacations. A certain amount of respite should be available to you at no cost. Again, your local ASA chapter should be able to assist you in locating it. Don't assume that a respite worker will understand your child's needs without guidance from you, even if the worker has been screened and trained.

5.   Find a good lawyer who understands and has experience in disability law. Learn what legal rights your child has to education, treatment, guardianship, and SSI benefits.

6.   Get to know the credentials of caregivers. Ask what kind of training they have had in the field of autism. Did they learn what they know in a one- or two-day workshop, or have they had extensive training? How many children with autism have they worked with in the past? In short, ascertain if they have proper certification, education, and experience for working with individuals with autism. If they don't, find caregivers who do, or demand that your school system finds them.

7. Be wary of cures. If it sounds too good to be true, it probably is. Ask to see scientific reports from professional journals supporting the technique. Be wary of any proof offered that is solely based on affidavits of satisfied clients.

8. Find places of acceptance where you will not receive critical looks or need to explain your child's behavior (e.g., places of worship, gatherings of family or friends, or certain restaurants).

9. Develop an identity separate from that of being the parent of a child with autism. Don't let this disorder consume you.

10. Celebrate your victories.

REFERENCES

Adrien, J. L., Faure, M., Perrot, A., Hameury, L., Garreau, B., Bertheleny, C., & Sauvage, D. (1991). Autism and family home movies: Preliminary findings. *Journal of Autism and Developmental Disorders, 21*(1), 43-49.

Akerley, M. (1988). What's in a name? In E. E. Schopler, & G. B. Mesibov (Eds.), *Diagnosis and assessment in autism* (pp. 59-67). New York: Plenum.

Amenta, C. A., III. (1992). *Russell is extra special: A book about autism for children*. New York: Magination Press.

American Psychiatric Association. (1994). *Diagnostic and statistical manual of mental disorders* (4th ed.) (DSM-IV). Washington, DC: Author.

Autism Society of America. (1990). *High-functioning adolescents with autism* [Cassette recording of proceedings of an Autism Society of America conference]. Houston, TX: Educational Audio Recording Service.

Autism Society of America. (1991). *America's funniest stories about ourselves and our kids with autism* [Cassette recording of proceedings of an Autism Society of America conference]. Houston, TX: Educational Audio Recording Service.

Autism Society of America. (1992). *How to survive with a child with autism in the family* [Cassette recording of proceedings of an Autism Society of America conference]. Houston, TX: Educational Audio Recording Service.

Autism Society of America. (n.d.). *Autism Fact Sheet*. Bethesda, MD: Author.

Bannerman, D. J., Sheldon, J. B., Sherman, J. A., & Harchik, A. E. (1990). Balancing the right to habilitate with the right to personal liberties: The rights of people with developmental disabilities to eat too many donuts and take a nap. *Journal of Applied Behavioral Analysis, 23*(1), 79-89.

Bell, D. (1992). *Faces at the Bottom of the Well*. NY: Basic Books.

Bourne, R., & Schweitzer, R. (1990). The impact of chronic childhood illness on family stress: A comparison between autism and cystic fibrosis. *Journal of Clinical Psychology, 46*, 722-730.

Burke, M. L., Hainsworth, M. A., Eakes, G., & Lindgren, C. L. (1992). Current knowledge and research on chronic sorrow: A foundation for inquiry. *Death Studies, 16,* 231-245.

Campbell, M., Anderson, L. T., Small, A. M., Lynch, N. S., & Choroco, M. C. (1990). Naltrexone in autistic children: A double-blind and placebo-controlled study. *Psychopharmacology Bulletin, 26,* 130-135.

Caramagno, L. (1992, Spring). A diagnostic work-up for autism. *The Advocate* (newsletter of the Autism Society of America, Inc.), pp. 13-14.

Castelloe, P., & Dawson, G. (1993). Subclassification of children with autism and pervasive developmental disorder: A questionnaire based on Wing's subgrouping scheme. *Journal of Autism and Developmental Disorders, 23,* 229 - 241.

Changes requested in DSM-IV. (1991, Fall). *The Advocate* (newsletter of the Autism Society of America, Inc.), p. 14.

Charlop, M. H., Kurtz, P. F., & Casey, F. G. (1990). Using aberrant behaviors as reinforcers for autistic children. *Journal of Applied Behavioral Analysis, 23,* 163-181.

Christopher, W., & Christopher, B. (1989). *Mixed blessings,* Nashville: Abington Press.

Coggins, T. E., & Frederickson, R. (1988). The communication role of a highly frequent repetitive utterance in the conversation of an autistic boy, *Journal of Autism and Developmental Disorders, 18,* 687-694.

Cutler, B. C., & Kozloff, M. A. (1987). Living with autism: Effects on families and family needs. In D. J. Cohen, & A. M. Donnellan (Eds.), *Handbook of autism and pervasive developmental disorders* (pp. 513-527). New York: John Wiley and Sons.

DeMeyer, M. K., & Goldberg, P. (1984). Family needs of the autistic adolescent. In E. Schopler, & G. B. Mesibov (Eds.), *Autism in adolescents and adults* (pp. 225-249). New York: Plenum Press.

Dillon, K. M. (1988, Fall). Autistic humor or name that windshield wiper. *The Advocate* (newsletter of the Autism Society of America, Inc.), p. 6.

Dillon, K. M. (1993), Facilitated communication, autism, and ouija. *Skeptical Inquirer, 17*, 281-287.

Egel, A. L. (1989). Finding the right educational program. In M. D. Powers (Ed.), *Children with autism: A parents' guide* (pp. 169-202). Rockville, MD: Woodbine House, Inc.

Eikiseth, S., & Lovaas, O. I., (1992). The autistic label and its potentially detrimental effect on the child's treatment. *Journal of Behavior Therapy and Experimental Psychiatry, 23*, 151-157.

Fisman, S., & Wolf, L. (1991). The handicapped child: Psychological effects of parental, marital, and sibling relationships. *Psychiatric Clinics of North America, 14*, 199-217.

Fotheringham, J. B. (1991). Autism: Its primary psychological and neural deficit. *Canadian Journal of Psychiatry, 36*, 686-692.

Friedrich, W. N., Cohen, D. S., & Wilturner, L. T. (1988). Specific beliefs as moderator variables in maternal coping with mental retardation. *Children's Health Care, 17*, 40-44.

Frith, U. (1993). Autism. *Scientific American, 268*(6), 108-114.

Gill, M. J., & Harris, S. L. (1991). Hardiness and social support as predictors of psychological discomfort in mothers of children with autism. *Journal of Autism and Developmental Disorders, 21*, 407-416.

Gillberg, C. (1991). Debate and argument: Is autism a pervasive developmental disorder? *Journal of Child Psychology and Psychiatry and Allied Disciplines, 32*, 1169-1170.

Greenhouse, L. (1992, September 20). The end of racism and other fables. *The New York Times Book Review*, p. 7.

Greenough, B. S. (1989). Foreword to M. D. Powers (Ed.), *Children with autism: A parents' guide* (pp. v-vii). Rockville, MD: Woodbine House, Inc.

Handen, B. L. (1993). Pharmacotherapy in mental retardation and autism. *School Psychology Review, 22*, 162-183.

Happe, F. & Frith, U. (1991). Is autism a pervasive developmental disorder? Debate and argument: How useful is the PDD label? *Journal of Child Psychology and Psychiatry and Allied Disciplines, 32*, 1167-1168.

Hart, C. (1989). *Without reason: A family copes with two generations of autism.* New York: Signet.

Hart, C. A. (1993). *A parent's guide to autism: Answers to the most common questions*. New York: Pocket Books.

Holmes, N., & Carr, J. (1991). The pattern of care in families of adults with a mental handicap: A comparison between families of autistic adults and Down syndrome adults. *Journal of Autism and Developmental Disorders, 21*, 159-176.

Holroyd, S., & Baron-Cohen, S. (1993). How far can people with autism go in developing a theory of mind? *Journal of Autism and Developmental Disorders, 23*, 379-385.

Hoppes, K., & Harris, S. L. (1990). Perceptions of child attachment and maternal gratification in mothers of children with autism and Down syndrome. *Journal of Clinical Child Psychology, 19*, 365-370.

Janoff-Bulman, R. (1992). *Shattered assumptions: Toward a new psychology of trauma*. New York: Free Press.

Johnson, M. (Producer), & Levinson, B. (Director). (1988). *Rainman* [Film]. Culver City, CA: MGM/UA Home Video.

Kanner. L. (1943). Autistic disturbances of affective contact. *Nervous Child, 2*, 217-250.

Kanner, L. (1992). Follow-up study of 11 autistic children originally reported in 1943. Reprinted in *Focus on Autistic Behavior, 7*(5), 1-11.

Kobayashi, R., Murata, T., & Yoshinaga, K. (1992). A follow-up study of 201 children with autism in Kyushu and Yamaguchi areas, Japan. *Journal of Autism and Developmental Disorders, 22*, 395-411.

Koegel, R. L., & Mentis, M. (1985). Motivation in autism: Can they or won't they? *Journal of Child Psychology and Psychiatry and Allied Disciplines, 26*, 185-191.

Koegel, R. L., Schreibman, L., Loos, L. M., Dirlich-Wilhelm, H., Dunlap, G., Robbins, F. R., & Plienis, A. J. (1992). Consistent stress profiles in mothers of children with autism. *Journal of Autism and Developmental Disorders, 22*, 206-216.

Konstantareas, M. M., & Homatidis, S. (1989). Assessing child symptom severity and stress in parents of autistic children. *Journal of Child Psychology and Psychiatry and Allied Disciplines, 30*, 459-470.

Kushner, H. S. (1981). *When bad things happen to good people.* New York: Avon Books.

Lovaas, O. I. (1981). *The me book: Teaching developmentally disabled children.* Austin, TX: Pro-Ed, Inc.

Lovaas, O. I. (1987). Behavioral treatment and normal educational and intellectual functioning in young autistic children. *Journal of Consulting and Clinical Psychology, 55,* 3-9.

Lovaas, I. (1990, September 24). Letter to colleagues in autism research and treatment.

Lovaas, O. I. (1991, September). *Partners for progress: Treatment and training.* Address presented at a conference entitled Partners for Progress: Treatment and Training, Cherry Hill, NJ.

Lovaas, O. I., & Smith, T. (1994). Intensive and long-term treatments for clients with destructive behaviors. In T. Thompson, & D. B. Gray (Eds.), *Destructive behavior in developmental disabilities: Diagnosis and treatment* (pp. 243-260). Thousand Oaks, CA: Sage Publications.

Lyle, K. L. (1992, March 2). A gentle way to die. *Newsweek,* p. 14.

Maurice, C. (1993). *Let me hear your voice: A family's triumph over autism.* New York: Knopf.

McEachin, J. J., Smith, T., & Lovaas, O. I. (1993). Long-term outcome for children with autism who received early intensive behavioral treatment. *American Journal on Mental Retardation, 97,* 359-372.

Mulick, J. A., Jacobson, J. W., & Kobe, F. H. (1993). Anguished silence and helping hands: Autism and facilitated communication. *Skeptical Inquirer, 17,* 270-280.

Otero, P. (1982). The Battlefield. *The Advocate 14 (4),* 6. Reprinted in Sposato, B. (Comp.). (n.d.). *A Collection of Writings from Advocate,* 1979-1989. Lincoln, NE: Autism Society of Nebraska, Inc.

Ousley, O. Y., & Mesibov, G. B. (1991). Sexual attitudes and knowledge of high-functioning adolescents and adults with autism. *Journal of Autism and Developmental Disorders, 21,* 471-481.

Phelps, L., & Grabowski, J. (1991). Autism: A communique for the school psychologist. *School Psychologist International, 12,* 299-314.

Popper, C. W., & Steingard, R. J. (1994), Disorders usually first diagnosed in infancy, childhood, or adolescence. In R. E. Hales, S. C. Yudofsky, & J. A. Talbott (Eds.), *The American Psychiatric Press Textbook of Psychiatry* (2nd ed.) (pp. 729-831). Washington, DC: American Psychiatric Press, Inc.

Post, C. (1993, Spring). Low functioning in a high functioning world. *The Advocate* (newsletter of the Autism Society of America, Inc.), p. 9.

Powers, M. D. (Ed.). (1989a). *Children with autism: A parents' guide*. Rockville, MD: Woodbine House, Inc.

Powers, M. D. (1989b). What is autism? In M. D. Powers (Ed.), *Children with autism, A parents' guide* (pp. 1-29). Rockville, MD: Woodbine House, Inc.

Rando, T. A. (1986). The unique issues and impact of the death of a child. In T. A. Rando (Ed.), *Parental loss of a child* (pp. 5-43). Champaign, IL: Research Press Co.

Rincover, A., Newsom, C. D., Lovaas, O. I., & Koegel, R. L. (1977). Some motivational properties of sensory stimulation in psychotic children. *Journal of Experimental Child Psychology*, *24*, 312-323.

Ritvo, E. R., Brothers, A. M., Freeman, B. J., & Pingree, C. (1988). Eleven possibly autistic parents. *Journal of Autism and Developmental Disorders*, *18*, 139-143.

Ritvo, E. R., Mason-Brothers, A., Freeman, B. J., Pingree, C., Janson, W. R., McMahon, W. M., Petersen, P. B., Jorde, L. B., Mo, A., & Ritvo, A. (1990). The UCLA and University of Utah epidemiologic survey of autism: The etiology of rare diseases. *American Journal of Psychiatry*, *147*, 1614 - 1621.

Rodrigue, J. R., Morgan, S. B., & Geffken, G. R. (1992). Psychosocial adaptation of fathers of children with autism, Down syndrome, and normal development. *Journal of Autism and Developmental Disorders*, *22*, 249-263.

Rutter, M., (1991). Autism: Pathways from syndrome definition to pathogenesis. *Comprehensive Mental Health Care*, *1* (1), 5-26.

Sacks, O. (1990). *Awakenings*. New York: Harper Perennial.

Sage, D. L. (Writer, Producer, & Director). (1984). *Madness*, part 7 of an 8-part PBS Television Series, *The Brain*. Washington, DC: The Annenberg/CPB Collection.

Sahley, T. L., & Pankssepp, J. (1987). Brain opioids and autism: An updated analysis of possible linkages. *Journal of Autism and Developmental Disorders, 17,* 201-215.

Sanua, V. D. (1986a). A comparative study of opinions of U.S.A. and European professionals on the etiology of infantile autism. *The International Journal of Social Psychiatry, 32,* 16-30.

Sanua, V. D. (1986b). The organic etiology of infantile autism: A critical review of the literature. *International Journal of Neurosciences, 30,* 195-225.

Schopler, E., Reichler, R. J., & Renner, B. R. (1986). *The childhood autism rating scale (CARS),* Los Angeles: Western Psychological Services.

Seligman, J., & Chideya, F. (1992, September 21). Horror story or big hoax. *Newsweek,* p. 75.

Siegel, B., Pliner, C., Escher, J, & Elliott, G. R. (1988). How children with autism are diagnosed: Difficulties in identification of children with multiple developmental delays. *Developmental and Behavioral Pediatrics, 9,* 199-204.

Spiker, D., Lotspeich, L., Hallmayer, J., Kraemer, H. C., & Ciaranello, R. D. (1993). Failure to find cytogenetic abnormalities in autistic children whose parents grew up near plastic manufacturing sites. *Journal of Autism and Developmental Disorders, 23,* 681-682.

Spitzer, R. L., Gibbon, M., Skodol, A. E., Williams, J. B. W., & First, M. B. (1994), *DSM-IV Case Book* (4th ed.). Washington, DC: American Psychiatric Press, Inc.

Sposato, B. (1995, March-April). *The Advocate* (newsletter of the Autism Society of America, Inc.).

Sposato, B. (Comp.). (n.d.). *A Collection of Writings from The Advocate, 1979-1989.* Lincoln, NE: Autism Society of Nebraska, Inc.

Szatmari, P., Bartolucci, G., Bremner, R., Bond, S., & Rich, S. (1989). A follow-up study of high-functioning autistic children. *Journal of Autism and Developmental Disorders, 19,* 213-225.

Toxic waste site: link to autism? (1990). *Autism Research Review International, 4*(4), 6.

Treffert, D. A. (1989). *Extraordinary people: Understanding "idiot savants", spectacularly gifted musicians, artists, calculators, and mneumonists who have severe mental disabilities.* New York: Harper & Row.

Venter, A., Lord, C., & Schopler, E. (1992). A follow-up study of high-functioning autistic children. *Journal of Child Psychology and Psychiatry and Allied Disciplines, 33*, 489-507.

Volkmar, F. R. (1989). Medical problems, treatments, and professionals. In M. D. Powers (Ed.), *Children with autism: A parents' guide* (pp. 55-77). Rockville, MD: Woodbine House, Inc.

Volkmar, F. R., & Cohen, D. J. (1985). The experience of infantile autism: A first-person account by Tony W. *Journal of Autism and Developmental Disorders, 15*, 47-54.

Volkmar, F. R., & Cohen, D. J. (1988). Classification and diagnosis of childhood autism. In E. Schopler, & G.B. Mesibov (Eds.), *Diagnosis and assessment in autism* (pp. 71 - 89). New York: Plenum.

Volkmar, F. R., & Cohen, D. J. (1991). Debate and argument: The utility of the term Pervasive Developmental Disorder. *Journal of Child Psychology and Psychiatry and Allied Disciplines, 32*, 1171-1172.

Walters, A. C., Barrett, R. P., Feinstein, C., Mercurio, A., & Hole, W. T. (1990). A case report of naltrexone treatment of self-injury and social withdrawal in autism. *Journal of Autism and Developmental Disorders, 20*, 169-176.

Williams, D. (1992). *Nobody nowhere.* New York: Times Books/Random House.

Williams, D. (1994). *Somebody somewhere.* New York: Times Books/Random House.

Wing, L. (1985). *Autistic child: A guide for parents and professionals* (2nd ed.). New York: Brunner/Mazel.

Wing, L. (1988). The continuum of autistic characteristics. In E. Schopler, & G. M. Mesibov (Eds.), *Diagnosis and assessment in autism* (pp. 91-110). New York: Plenum.

Yirmiya, N., & Sigman, M. (1991). High-functioning individuals with autism: Diagnosis, empirical findings, and theoretical issues. *Clinical Psychology Review, 11*, 669-683.

Zilbovicius, M., Garreau, B., Tzourio, N., Mazoyer, B., Bruck, B., Martinot, J., Raynaud, C., Samson, Y., Syrota, A., & LeLord, G. (1992). Regional cerebral blood flow in childhood autism: A SPECT study. *American Journal of Psychiatry, 149*, 924-930.

GLOSSARY

ALZHEIMER'S DISEASE. An age-related disease characterized by cognitive impairment, especially memory loss.

ANOXIA. Oxygen deprivation.

APGAR SCORE. A numerical estimation of the condition of an infant a few minutes after birth (highest score = 10).

ASPERGER'S DISORDER. An impairment in social interaction and range of interests and behaviors with no delay in language or cognitive development or problems with self-help skills or curiosity about the environment.

AUDITORY TRAINING. An unsubstantiated technique which claims to desensitize a child to painful or distracting sounds.

BEHAVIOR THERAPY. The systematic use of reinforcers to modify behavior (also called Applied Behavioral Analysis and Behavior Modification).

CHILDHOOD DISINTEGRATIVE DISORDER. A pervasive developmental disorder characterized by normal development up to 2 years of age, followed by significant loss of language skills, social skills, bowel or bladder control, ability to play, or motor skills.

CHILDHOOD SCHIZOPHRENIA. A rare mental disorder that usually develops after years of normal development, characterized by delusions, hallucinations, disorganized speech or behavior, or lack of usual behaviors and emotions.

CHRONIC SORROW. A long-lasting state of sadness or grief.

DELUSION. A belief maintained in the face of incontrovertible evidence.

DEPARTMENT OF MENTAL RETARDATION (DMR). A state agency designed to meet the needs of the mentally retarded.

DOWN SYNDROME. A congenital disorder which results in mental retardation and particular facial features.

ECHOLALIA. A parroting back of speech (can be immediate or delayed).

ELECTROENCEPHALOGRAM (EEG). A brain wave recording.

ENCEPHALITIS. An inflammation of the brain.

FACILITATED COMMUNICATION (FC). A controversial technique in which the instructor assists the learner to communicate by guiding the learner's finger, hand, or wrist on a communication board or computer.

FENFLURAMINE. A drug used to treat autism by lowering serotonin levels. It was first tried in the early 1980s, often with disappointing results.

FRAGILE X SYNDROME. A condition in which a part of the X chromosome is defective.

GUARDIAN. A person legally appointed to manage the affairs of an individual.

HABITUATE. To lessen or cease responding to a stimulus over repeated exposure.

HALLUCINATION. A perception without an external stimulus (e.g., hearing voices when no one is speaking).

HARDINESS. Extent to which a person feels in control of the environment, sees meaning in life, and feels challenged by problems.

HIGH-FUNCTIONING. An imprecise term describing individuals with autism who are verbal and of higher intelligence.

HYDROCELE. An accumulation of fluid in the testes.

INTELLIGENCE QUOTIENT (IQ). A score, derived from a standardized test, which gives a measure of a person's ability to think and reason.

KANNER THEORY. A theory derived in 1943 by Leo Kanner, a child psychiatrist, describing the common characteristics of what he called early infant autism.

KARYOTYPE. A chromosome picture.

LEARNED HELPLESSNESS. A state of passivity that can develop after a person experiences multiple failures or uncontrollable events.

MENTAL ILLNESS. A psychological dysfunction, which may or may not have a physical origin, that causes considerable distress to the individual and/or to others.

MENTAL RETARDATION. A condition of low intellectual functioning, usually defined as an IQ of less than 70.

NALTREXONE. A promising, experimental drug treatment for autism that counteracts the effect of the natural opiates of the brain.

OCCUPATIONAL THERAPIST. A person who specializes in treating physical defects or problems in adaptive skills by means of work or related activities.

PAROTID GLAND. One of the salivary glands.

PERSEVERATION. Prolonged repetition of a word or phrase.

PERVASIVE DEVELOPMENTAL DISORDER (PDD). A number of mental disorders characterized by many severe impairments in development.

PHENYLKETONURIA. A hereditary metabolic disorder in which there is a deficiency of phenylalanine hydroxylase.

REFRIGERATOR MOTHER. An erroneous notion, once commonly considered true, that cold, unloving parenting caused autism.

REINFORCER. A consequence of a behavior which increases the likelihood that the behavior will be repeated.

RETT'S DISORDER. A pervasive developmental disorder found only in females, characterized by normal early period followed by head growth deceleration, loss of purposeful hand skills (replaced by hand-wringing or hand-washing movements), psychomotor retardation, and severe problems with language development.

RESPITE WORKER. A person hired to watch a dependent person in order to provide the family a period of relief or rest.

RUBELLA. German measles.

SAVANT. A person who shows exceptional ability in a particular area.

SELF-INJURIOUS BEHAVIOR. Harmful physical actions done by an individual to himself or herself.

SENSORY INTEGRATION. A therapy that uses physical activities to help children with autism regulate their responses to input from different sensory systems. Some programs, such as the Doman-Delcato Patterning Technique, are of questionable validity.

SPECIAL EDUCATION (SPED). Education designed for the disabled and for people with unusual needs.

STEREOTYPY. Prolonged purposeless repetition of a behavior.

SUPPLEMENTAL SECURITY INCOME (SSI). A government benefit that provides income to the disabled.

SWEAT TEST. A medical test to measure the levels of sodium and chloride in sweat. It is used to diagnose cystic fibrosis in children.

TEMPORAL LOBE EPILEPSY. Recurrent seizures originating in the temporal lobe of the brain (a part of the brain that has also been implicated in the etiology of autism).

TEGRETAL. An anticonvulsant drug.

TOURETTE'S SYNDROME. A disorder which begins in childhood, characterized by single or multiple tics involving muscle contractions and/or vocalizations that are brief, repetitive, and purposeless.

TOXEMIA. A condition in which the blood contains poisonous substances.

TUBEROS SCLEROSIS. A medical condition involving the nervous system and the skin.

VESTIBULAR. Pertaining to the physical sense of balance.

VITAMIN B6-MAGNESIUM COMBINATION. A controversial megavitamin regimen for treating autism, advocated by psychologist Bernard Rimland.

WERNICKE'S AREA. An area of the brain which controls speech.

WECHSLER INTELLIGENCE SCALE FOR CHILDREN-REVISED (WISC-R). An IQ test for children (now in its 4th edition).

XANAX. An anti-anxiety drug.

AUTHOR AND SUBJECT INDEX